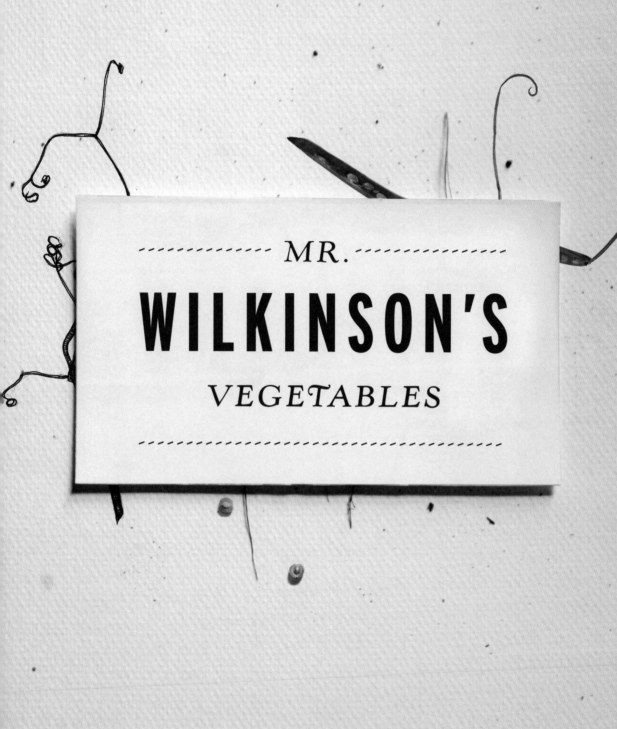

MR.
WILKINSON'S
VEGETABLES

MR.
WILKINSON'S

VEGETABLES

A COOKBOOK TO CELEBRATE THE GARDEN

MATT WILKINSON

BLACK DOG
& LEVENTHAL
PUBLISHERS
NEW YORK

Thank you so much for picking up this book and reading it.
I have many cookbooks and not one person has thanked me for buying,
reading or using them—so thank you. I hope that as you read it, you will
be inspired by the same love of good food that inspires me every day.

CONTENTS

A GREEN THUMB

SO WHY A BOOK ON VEGETABLES, I HEAR YOU ASK

It's quite simple. Thinking about the vegetables first is how I cook. I look to the season we are in to get my ideas about what will be on the menu where I'm working or what I will eat at home that night, and there is no better way to find out what is in season than looking at the often underrated vegetable. I build my dish around what vegetables are in season because this is when they will be the cheapest, most readily available and, most importantly, taste the best—and surely this has to be the most important factor when cooking. It's a simple concept that when things are in season they taste so much better … But, then, how have we lost this simple thought process to eating? Look at each season. In spring, I walk into the garden and I feel alive—there is a fresh and crisp feeling in the air and soil, the trees are budding and their leaves have sprung forth. When I harvest the beans or peas from their stalks, there is a zingy snap to them—whether cooked or raw they taste so sweet. In summer, the earth is warmed and the plants almost hot to touch; with careful watering, they stay alert as though they are ready for battle. Just close

your eyes and think of the smell of tomatoes— it's unmistakable and makes my mouth salivate waiting for the first bite. Autumn arrives and the mood around the garden softens, the plants are readying themselves for the cooler weather. The vegetable patch has had a great time; the basil, sorrel, spinach and Swiss chard are looking magnificent and the butternut squash and zucchini are still going great guns. When winter arrives, I add the year's compost and some manure to the soil and look at my blooming red cabbages that have been in the ground for so many months now. The broccoli is so alive and glowing such a deep green that I think I might harvest it for dinner tonight, and the salad leaves are crisp and so fresh.

Once I have decided what seasonal bounty to make the most of, and considered how the flavors will marry together, I then add the protein to my dish, usually meat or seafood, then some carbs if needed.

If you think back to times gone by, this was the way everyone had to eat. For most people, meat and seafood were not readily available, were too expensive or were hard to store (no fridges or freezers then). Over the past fifty years, technology has meant we can be a little lazy in our food thinking, with great cuts of meat and seafood on hand. Today a lot of people think about what protein they feel like eating—will it be beef or chicken, fish or pork? Then what starch will be added to bulk out the meal and, as a final touch, throw in a few vegetables. This is where I'm a little different with my veg-first approach. I hope you feel inspired, while reading this book, to try the old-fashioned method to choosing the vegetable first. Vegetables are so much more diverse in flavor, types and availability than any old piece of meat.

MY FAVORITE VEGETABLES?

You might also be wondering how I arrived at the list of vegetables included in this book. Well, I can't begin to tell you how hard it was to select them. (In fact there is even one vegetable in the book that I do at times detest. I'll leave that one for you to discover, kind of a *Where's Waldo* element to the book.) But let me tell you about some vegetables I didn't have room to include: the sweet, earthy and diverse celeriac (celery root) and its sweeter, sexier looking cousin, celery; the Welsh national emblem vegetable, the grand *ole* leek; two personal favorites of mine that have

the same ending name but come from different families—the delightful and thistle-looking globe artichoke and the earthier yet knobbly sunchoke; and lastly the glorious funghi family, which some of us hate but others love (technically not vegetables, although they too come first when I am planning a meal). Perhaps, one day, there will be book number two, where I could include these: *The Vegetables Mr. Wilkinson Forgot*.

However, this being said, twenty-three out of the twenty-four vegetables in this book I could not live without (and, in writing the book, I've come to appreciate even the one I had long disliked). I do hope you enjoy the recipes, the little history about them, how I grow them and what they mean to me. Growing, cooking and eating vegetables is healthy, better for the planet than a diet heavy in meat and, best of all, means meals full of flavor and diversity.

TWO ESSENTIAL TIPS

I'll take this opportunity to give you two cooking tips that I really think you will appreciate and incorporate into your culinary repertoire— whether it's for use with this book or any others you may have.

1. How frustrating do you find it when, after a meal, you have all the cooking dishes to clean up? Personally it annoys me. So simply clean as you go. Take time out of the cooking process to clean up after yourself and try to use the same pot or pan again if you can. Otherwise, if you have children, never mind—making them wash up is a good way for them to earn their keep.

2. This tip will help you immensely if you do it. Cooking should be fun, relaxed and certainly not a chore. If you follow these simple steps when looking at a recipe, I promise you, they will help you to be more organized and less stressed:

⁃ *After you have chosen the dish and recipe you would like to cook, sit down, have a cup of tea or glass of wine and have a pen and notepad at the ready.*

⁃ *Read the ingredients list and method thoroughly.*

⁃ *Have a sip of your chosen beverage, then read the recipe again.*

⁃ *Now, write out the ingredients list with measurements of those you need to go and buy.*

⁃ *Have another sip.*

⁃ *Now write out the method in your own words, not copying, but your own words.*

⁃ *Sip number three.*

⁃ *Then check that you have the correct ingredients, method and you know what you need to purchase.*

⁃ *Close the book and do not open it again. Use your notes to cook from. This helps for a few reasons. First, when you write the method in your own words you will understand it more clearly when following the steps. Second, you don't dirty your precious cookbook with cooking marks. And third, you are starting your own personal cookbook. You can adapt the recipes to your liking and they are at hand when and if you need them in the future.*

Try this out, it helped me immensely and will help you too.

TO MY LITTLE RAY OF SUNSHINE
FINN THOMAS AND YOUR BEAUTIFUL
MOTHER MY LOVE SHARLEE AND, OF COURSE,
QUINCY the DOG.

Flowering perennial /
lives up to 30 years.

NATIVE TO EUROPE,
NORTHERN AFRICA,
WESTERN ASIA

ARISES FROM A ROOT SYSTEM OF
FLESHY RHIZOMES. KNOWN AS THE CROWN.

The name "asparagus" comes from the Greek language meaning "sprout" or "shoot"

Let asparagus be the crown jewel of vegetables that you wait for every spring. The beautiful snap of the stalk when ripe, the crunch of it raw in a salad or delicately cooked.

ASPARAGUS

ASPARAGUS

I may harp on a lot about eating vegetables only when they are in season but honestly, wherever you are in the world, is there really any other vegetable that you would live without for a whole year, just waiting for the next brief season, except the beautiful asparagus?

THE CROWN JEWEL

Growing up in England, I remember eating asparagus when I was younger, but it wasn't until I moved to Scotland and started my career working for Martin Wishart that I realized how stunning fresh asparagus truly is, and I began to fully appreciate the luxury of it. It was almost a "truffle moment" for me—that amazing indescribable sensation when you smell and taste a real truffle for the first time. It was just like that when the first boxes of asparagus would arrive. The Scottish season was so fleeting—only a few weeks—but what it left me with was a deep appreciation for seasonality and why asparagus is so worth waiting for. Those few weeks were just wonderful.

And that's where the interesting point lies: it's so amazing in season, but so terrible out of season. It's woody, tasteless, limp and, on top of all that, bloody expensive! So why buy it? Why buy asparagus imported from Thailand? Why import it at all? Do we really need to be able to buy asparagus year round from the supermarket? I understand that people don't want to go through half the year without, say, the tomato, but asparagus? If you're just using it because you

have a recipe book that says "use asparagus," well, how about choosing a different recipe instead?

Surely we can wait? The flavor, the anticipation, the beautiful snap of the stalk when ripe, the crunch of it raw in a salad or delicately, respectfully cooked. Let asparagus be the crown jewel (fittingly it's got a lovely crown hat) of vegetables that you will wait just for spring to come around again so you can enjoy it.

The tip of the spear, if left to grow, will become a flower—just like the globe artichoke. It is a member of the lily family (and therefore related to the likes of onion, leek and garlic) and, though it originated in the Mediterranean, it has been naturalized all over the world. It grows wild in the salt marshes of Europe and Asia, but it was the Romans who first cultivated and domesticated it. It has always been considered the height of elegance and a favorite of kings and emperors. The Egyptians even gave bundles of it as offerings to their gods. It has been respected for its beauty and elegance for thousands of years, and I think we need to continue showing it that respect.

PREPARING AND COOKING

The asparagus season begins in early spring, and, if conditions are favorable, will continue through to early summer. Early in the season, you should be able to eat it just as it is. When it's young and fresh, you can eat it raw and it makes a lovely crudité, which works perfectly with bagna càuda (see page 149). But, as the season goes on, you should peel the stalk as the skin can become quite fibrous. You should also cut or snap off about 1 inch from the base of the stalk as it is quite woody and makes for unpleasant eating. By doing this you also have an indicator as to how fresh the asparagus is; if fresh, you should get a lovely "snap" when you break it. Listen for it. And if you think that all this peeling and trimming is wasteful, then think again. Asparagus is really quite an amazing vegetable—you can use all of it. The peelings and stalk remnants can be used to make a soup or purée, and the rest can be boiled, broil, stir-fried, steamed, baked, broiled, or any other way you can think of.

WHITE VERSUS GREEN

Now, I have never grown asparagus, and the reason for that is it takes such a long time from sowing to harvest. If you grow from seed, it will take three years before you get a crop. To fast-track the situation somewhat, you can buy one-year-old plants, called "crowns," from your nursery, which will reduce the growing time. I have been lucky enough, though, to be invited by Jo and Trevor Courtney to their property, organic Bridge Farm, near Koo Wee Rup, to see how they grow their asparagus. And it is a truly beautiful sight to see, the elegant stalks lined up in rows. The fern of the plant is almost prehistoric looking like some sort of bracken.

The Courtneys explained to me some of the many ways to grow white asparagus, which is exactly the same plant as green but has been grown under different conditions—it is starved of sunlight so that the chlorophyll within the plant (the chemical which makes it green) can't develop. This can be done by covering the emerging crowns with soil or, as some other farmers do, with black plastic to stop the sun reaching the plants. There is an ongoing argument with chefs and growers the world over as to which, out of the green or white, is a better product, with many saying that the white has a sweeter and more delicate flavor. But it's really up to you which one you prefer. Try them both and make up your mind.

TAKE A CHANCE

And the topic you thought I might not touch on. Will eating asparagus make your wee smell or not? Scientists aren't sure what the compound is in asparagus that can make some people's urine smell. It appears to be a genetic thing as to whether it affects you or even whether you can smell it if it does. Only around 50 per cent of the population can ... I say, "Who cares?" For something this delicious, it's worth taking the chance!

BLANCHED WHITE ASPARAGUS
WITH RICOTTA & BELGIAN ENDIVE

SERVES 2 AS AN ENTRÉE

If you do not have any almond and orange spiced crumb on hand, you can substitute croûtons.

This salad works beautifully with some sliced charcuterie meat too.

1 LARGE BUNCH THICK-STEMMED WHITE ASPARAGUS (OR 2 BUNCHES THIN-STEMMED)

1 RED BELGIAN ENDIVE, LEAVES SEPARATED AND WASHED

¼ TEASPOON DIJON MUSTARD

1 CUP ARUGULA, WASHED AND SPUN DRY

⅓ CUP EXTRA VIRGIN OLIVE OIL

⅓ CUP FRESH RICOTTA

SEA SALT AND FRESHLY GROUND BLACK PEPPER

1 QUANTITY ALMOND AND ORANGE SPICED CRUMB (SEE PAGE 278)

½ SMALL HEAD RADICCHIO, LEAVES SEPARATED, WASHED AND TORN

Snap off the bottom part of the stalk of the asparagus. Slice a little of one stem and eat to see if the asparagus is stringy in texture. If it is, peel the skin with a vegetable peeler starting from the crown down to the base of the stem. If it isn't, leave her well alone. Halve the asparagus widthways.

Cook the asparagus for 1–3 minutes, depending on the size, in a saucepan of salted boiling water until still a little firm. Drain and plunge into a bowl of icy cold water. Once cold, remove immediately from the water and put into a bowl.

Whisk together the mustard and olive oil and season with salt and pepper. Pour over the asparagus and mix until well coated.

Tear in the radicchio and add the Belgian endive and arugula. Gently break up the ricotta with a spoon and mix in half of it. Place onto plates, top with the rest of the ricotta, then pour over any remaining juices from the bowl. Sprinkle over a generous amount of the spiced crumb and serve.

PICKLED ASPARAGUS

→ FILLS 3 x 10½ FLUID OUNCE JARS

As a general rule, when it comes to pickling, it should be done when the produce is at its peak and is therefore cheaper. When it comes to pickling asparagus, I don't really follow that rule, though. I usually pickle different varieties of asparagus at the start of the season to preserve the first crop, which have skins that are really succulent and do not need peeling. Pickled asparagus is great as part of an anitpasti platter or added to salads when the fresh stuff is out of season.

6 BUNCHES ASPARAGUS

2 ⅓ CUPS WHITE WINE VINEGAR

1 ½ CUPS APPLE CIDER VINEGAR

¼ TEASPOON MUSTARD SEEDS

¼ TEASPOON CORIANDER SEEDS

¼ TEASPOON WHITE PEPPERCORNS

2 GARLIC CLOVES, THINLY SLICED

1 SHALLOT, THINLY SLICED

Preheat the oven to 275°F.

Wash and make sure your glass jars are odor-free and dry. Lay a jar on its side and measure the asparagus next to it, chopping off the bottom part of the stalks to fit the jars. (Discard the scraps or use to make asparagus soup or a salad.)

Quickly blanch the asparagus in a saucepan of salted boiling water, then drain and refresh in icy cold water. Once cool, take out and pat dry, then place into the jars, crown side up.

Put the vinegars in a saucepan and bring to a boil, then allow to cool. Divide the spices, garlic and shallot between each jar and pour over the vinegar, making sure the liquid completely covers the asparagus. Screw on the lids, place on a baking sheet and put into the oven for 10 minutes. Label and store in your cupboard for at least 1 week before using, but 3 months is better. Unopened jars will keep until the next season. Once opened, store in the fridge.

SALAD OF RAW ASPARAGUS, SKORDALIA, PROSCIUTTO & DUKKA

SERVES 4 AS AN ENTRÉE OR AS A SALAD TO SHARE

Such a quick and simple salad to make for lunch. You could replace the skordalia with a simple aïoli and the result would be just as delicious. You could also add a little shaved Parmesan, if you wished, and maybe even a perfectly poached egg to enhance the dish even more.

2 LARGE BUNCHES GREEN ASPARAGUS
(THICK-STEMMED PREFERABLY)

1 TABLESPOON FINE SEA SALT

8 SLICES PROSCIUTTO

3 TABLESPOONS EXTRA VIRGIN OLIVE OIL,
PLUS EXTRA TO SERVE

JUICE OF ½ LEMON

1 TABLESPOON CHOPPED BASIL,
PLUS EXTRA TO SERVE

1 TABLESPOON CHOPPED ITALIAN
PARSLEY, PLUS EXTRA TO SERVE

FRESHLY GROUND BLACK PEPPER

1 QUANTITY POTATO SKORDALIA
(SEE NOTE, PAGE 210)

2 TABLESPOONS DUKKA (SEE PAGE 278)

Using a mandoline, thinly slice the asparagus from the base to the crown, making long ribbons. Place in a large bowl, add the salt and let stand for 1 minute. Tear in the prosciutto, add the olive oil, lemon juice, basil and parsley and season with salt and pepper. Dollop some of the skordalia onto the plates, arrange the asparagus salad neatly on top and finish with a drizzle of olive oil, some more chopped herbs and a sprinkling of dukka.

HARVEST
IN 12-14 WEEKS

PEA PLANTS . CAN SELF POLLINATE

Peas are an annual
cool season crop

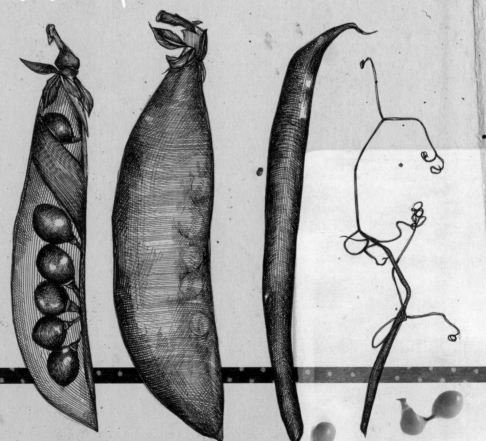

THE UNIVERSAL BEAN:

The Chinese have snake beans, the Indians love
dried beans in iconic dishes such as lentil dhal,
Italians love their cannellini and borlotti.

PROTEIN / FOLATE / IRON

BEANS & PEAS

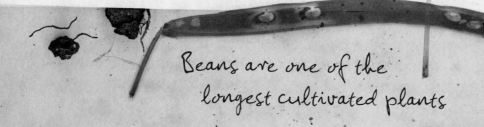

Beans are one of the
longest cultivated plants

BEANS & PEAS

I have to admit, for something that seems so simple, I'm really not the greatest at growing beans and peas—specifically sweet peas, runner beans and their ilk. But I have always been successful at growing fava beans. Beans and peas are vegetables so firmly entrenched in the English food lexicon that, when I was growing up, the standard question when you ordered anything at a pub was, "Peas or beans with that?" Peas being mushy peas and beans being baked beans. Beans and peas. Is it because they are readily available nearly all year round that we love them so much?

THE UNIVERSAL BEAN

They are what I like to think of as a "universal" vegetable, found in different guises as a staple foodstuff the whole world over. They are all members of what is known as the *Fabales* group, an order of flowering plants that include legumes, like chickpeas and lentils. And there are more varieties than you can count.

The Chinese have yard-long beans, which can grow up to a foot long. These are used throughout South-East Asia. Indians love to use both dried and fresh beans in their cuisine, in iconic dishes such as lentil dhal and chickpea curry. Middle Easterners have haricot blanc beans (better known to the rest of the world as "the bean found in your baked beans"), Italians love their cannellini and borlotti beans, and South Americans have the lima bean and red kidney bean varieties. All over the world, beans have been embraced and used fresh or dried. They are an extremely important part of the diets of people from developing nations, where meat may be too expensive or difficult to come by, as they are a valuable source of protein. Of course, this is precisely why vegetarians are big fans of beans: these powerhouses of protein are also a great source of many vitamins and minerals.

ALL GREEN BEANS ARE EQUAL

In the UK, where I hail from, we have become so accustomed to fine straight green beans (especially from areas like Kenya) that it is common practice to buy these beans judged on looks and not taste. We will discard a bean with a black spot, if it's not straight or has a bit of diversity in color. Watch people in the supermarket and see how they select fruit and veg, especially green beans. They always go for the best-looking ones and leave behind the less pretty ones … But when it comes to beans, they all have the same flavor.

GROWING FAVA BEANS

As I mentioned, I haven't had the greatest success growing beans and peas. I always set up a trellis and prepare the soil well but I can't seem to protect them from being attacked by bugs and being eaten alive. I don't like to spray as I've found this dries them out. So, for best tips on growing beans and peas, I will humbly direct you to look in gardening manuals.

But fava beans are a different story. Well, at least here, I can boast and say I have been very successful, getting two crops a year by seed saving and preparing the soil really well, with quite a bit of manure dug in. Plant your seeds quite close together, and then when the shoots get to knee height place some stakes into the ground for support. You don't need to tie the shoots to the stakes unless the plants are struggling to stay upright. Fava beans self-pollinate, in a similar way to corn, by the wind brushing them against one another, so they need to be close enough to each other to do that, otherwise you won't get any beans. But make sure they are far enough apart to allow some sunlight to penetrate in between.

By the time they have grown to shoulder height, they should start to produce lovely little pods. Now I like to think that these pods are like the beans' own sleeping bag and protector, which means I never buy beans or peas pre-podded. Imagine how nice it must be being a pea or bean in its sleeping bag, all snuggled up and tasty, then without warning being podded out into the world! And then put into the fridge as well. They go all dry and start to shrivel. This is why I always buy them still in their pods. It may take you a few more minutes to get dinner on the table but it is worth it to only pod them just before cooking.

PESKY EARWIGS

In terms of pests and blights there has only been one enemy I have had attacking my fava bean crop and that is earwigs. Earwigs just love fava beans. And the only way to know for sure if you have earwigs is to go out late at night with a flashlight and look for the little beggars. They hide away during the day, but catch them by surprize at night and you'll be amazed how many there can be attacking your broadies! I have two good tips for this. Place some linseed oil in a plastic container with a lid and pierce some large holes in it, then place it in the garden near the beans— the earwigs (and also some other pests) will be attracted to the oil and will drop themselves into the container. The other method is to use egg cartons. Place five half-dozen egg cartons stacked together and place in and around your crop— earwigs love to squeeze into tight, dark places and will find the nooks of the cartons irresistible. First thing every morning, empty each egg carton over a bucket of water. Keep doing this for a week and you should have got rid of enough of the little buggers to stop the damage to the plants.

NITROGEN FIXERS

Remember too that growing beans and peas is highly beneficial for your garden beds as a whole as the nitrogen stock in their roots is very good for your soil. Once you have harvested the entire bean crop, don't be tempted to pull out the plant straight away. Just leave them for a couple of weeks to die in the ground. They may not look great in your garden but the benefits are enormous. After they have died, cut about 2 inches from the base of the stalk and discard the rest of the plant. Dig the remaining stalk and roots right in and around, and really turn the soil over to release the nitrogen into the soil. This will really improve the soil for whatever you choose to plant into that bed next.

BAKED BEANS

SERVES 6

What is a cupboard or English breakfast without baked beans? Nothing.
So here is my recipe that we have on the menu at my restaurant Pope Joan.

⅔ CUP OLIVE OIL	½ TEASPOON GROUND TURMERIC
1 WHITE ONION, SLICED	2 TABLESPOONS TOMATO PASTE
1 TEASPOON SMOKED PAPRIKA	½ CUP SUGAR (ANY TYPE)
1 TEASPOON FRESHLY GROUND BLACK PEPPER	1 CUP RED WINE VINEGAR
1 TEASPOON FINE SEA SALT	2 x 14 OUNCE CANS CRUSHED TOMATOES
1 TEASPOON GROUND ALLSPICE	1 CAN OF WATER (USE AN EMPTY TOMATO CAN)
1 TEASPOON GROUND CUMIN	1 POUND 10 OUNCES CANNED COOKED WHITE BEANS (SEE NOTE)

Heat the olive oil in a saucepan (measuring at least 10 ½ inches in diameter by 4 inches deep) over medium heat. Add the onion and gently sweat. Once the onion has started to go translucent, add all the spices and cook out for 4 minutes. Add the tomato paste and cook out for 3 minutes. Add the sugar and vinegar and reduce by one-third or until sticky.

Add the tomatoes and water and bring to a boil. Continue to cook for 5 minutes on full heat, stirring continuously.

Turn the heat back down to medium, add the beans and cook until the beans have started to absorb the tomato and flavors of the sauce, about 15–25 minutes.

I serve the beans in little tins placed in the middle of the table for a bit of fun at breakfast with generously buttered slices of toast (you may want to peel the labels off the canned tomatoes and use them for serving in). The beans will keep refrigerated for up to 1 week.

Note You can use 2 x 13 ounce cans cooked white beans (cannellini or haricot), drained and rinsed, or 1 pound 10 ounces cooked dried white beans. If using the latter, soak 14 ounces of dried white beans in plenty of water, then drain and cook in boiling water for 30 minutes or until tender.

CRUSHED FAVA BEAN & LENTILS, GOAT CHEESE & PEAR

SERVES 2 AS A SALAD TO SHARE

I'm a fanatic about keeping fava beans in their "sleeping bags" or pods until just before cooking, but to double pod or not to double pod, now that is the question. If the beans are small and have just come in season, I'd keep them in their skins, otherwise, if they're slightly older and bigger, blanch and pod them.

½ BUNCH OF BABY BEETS, TOPPED AND TAILED

⅓ CUP RED WINE VINEGAR

10 ½ OUNCES PODDED FAVA BEANS (SEE NOTE)

½ CUP COOKED TINY BLUE-GREEN LENTILS (SEE PAGE 276), AT ROOM TEMPERATURE

1 PEAR (I LIKE TO USE RIPE WILLIAM PEARS FOR THIS SALAD)

¼ CUP ROUGHLY CHOPPED WALNUTS

3 TABLESPOONS WHITE BALSAMIC VINEGAR

3 TABLESPOONS EXTRA VIRGIN OLIVE OIL

3 TABLESPOONS CHOPPED ITALIAN PARSLEY

1 ¾ OUNCES BABY RED CHARD LEAVES, TRIMMED

1 PUNNET (ABOUT 2 OUNCES) MUSTARD CRESS, TRIMMED

SEA SALT AND FRESHLY GROUND BLACK PEPPER

1 ⅔ CUPS SOFT, FRESH GOAT CHEESE OR FROMAGE BLANC

Place the beets, red wine vinegar and 2 cups of water in a saucepan and bring to a boil, then reduce to a simmer and cook for 35–45 minutes or until tender. Remove from the heat and allow to sit in the liquid until they are cool enough to handle, then peel off their skins with your fingers (you may like to put on gloves to keep your hands from going purple). Discard the liquid. Halve the beets and set aside.

Place 3 cups of water and some salt in a clean saucepan and bring to a boil. Add the podded fava beans and cook for 2 minutes. Drain, refresh under cold water, then peel off their skins, place the beans in a large bowl and lightly crush with a fork. Add the lentils.

Cut the pear into quarters, then finely dice and add to the fava bean mixture. Add the walnuts, white balsamic vinegar, olive oil, parsley, baby red chard and mustard cress (but reserve some of the chard and cress for garnishing) and season with salt and pepper. Toss gently to combine.

To plate, spoon a little of the goat cheese onto a serving plate, arrange the beet halves on the goat cheese, then gently top with some of the fava bean mixture. Finish with a few spoonfuls more goat cheese and garnish with the reserved baby chard and mustard cress.

Note To get 10 ½ ounces podded fava beans you'll need about 2 pounds 4 ounces of beans in their pods.

PEA & MASCARPONE PLIN WITH SAGE & BUTTER SAUCE

SERVES 4–6

In October 2010 I was lucky enough to be an Australian delegate for Slow Food Melbourne at the legendary food conference Terra Madre in Turin, Piedmont, Italy. It was at the festival's Italian food Mecca called Eataly, housed in an old Fiat car workshop, that I was introduced to the mighty plin, essentially rough ravioli. Traditionally, plin is a very egg-yolky pasta filled with ground rabbit, pork and veal in a kind of ravioli shape. I have adapted the plin and made it with a vegetarian filling here, which I think is just as good, and served it with the same butter and sage sauce.

The Piedmontese style of pasta is much more egg yolky than anywhere else I know and, like bread, the recipe for pasta varies from region to region and country to country. I have accumulated many pasta recipes that are used to make different shapes and sizes, and the recipe below is a great one for plin, ravioli and tortellini. If you are wanting to make spaghetti or linguini, say, I'd suggest you use a recipe with less egg yolk in it (I'd try a recipe from Giorgio Locatelli's Made in Italy).

PASTA

7 ½ OUNCES EGG YOLK (ABOUT 13) (SEE NOTE)

1 ⅔ CUPS BREAD FLOUR

PEA AND MASCARPONE FILLING

1 ¾ CUPS FROZEN PEAS (YES, YES, I DO USE FROZEN PEAS)

⅔ CUP MASCARPONE

1 TABLESPOON FINELY CHOPPED CHIVES

SEA SALT AND FRESHLY GROUND BLACK PEPPER

TO SERVE

1 CUP BUTTER, DICED

1 ½ TABLESPOONS EXTRA VIRGIN OLIVE OIL

30 BABY SAGE LEAVES
(OR 15 NORMAL LEAVES, ROUGHLY CHOPPED)

⅔ CUP FRESH PEAS, PODDED

2 TABLESPOONS PASTA COOKING WATER

2 CUPS ARUGULA, PICKED AND WASHED (OPTIONAL)

1 CUP FINELY GRATED PARMESAN

For the pasta, add the egg yolk and flour to a food processor or the bowl of an electric mixer and slowly combine. It may seem dry initially but keep slowly working the dough and when a few crumbs are left in the base, turn the dough out onto a clean work surface and punch down until the yolk and flour are completely combined, about 5 minutes. Wrap in plastic wrap and set aside for 2 hours.

For the pea and mascarpone filling, cook the peas in salted boiling water for 3½ minutes. Drain and purée in a food processor until mushy. Scrape out into a bowl, fold in the mascarpone and chives and season with salt and pepper. Cover and chill for 30 minutes to firm up.

To make the plin, traditionally they are rolled out by hand but I use a pasta machine. The plin will take about 1 hour to make. Divide the pasta into quarters. Work with one-quarter at a time and cover the other pieces of pasta dough with a tea towel. Flatten the dough a little on a lightly floured work surface with a rolling pin so it will fit through the pasta machine. The widest setting on my pasta machine at home is number 7, so I roll the pasta through that setting twice, then I go down two notches at a time, rolling the pasta through each notch twice. The last notch you should roll at is number 2.

The length of the pasta should be around 35½ inches. Cut the sheet in half and lay one half above the other. Now fold the bottom part of one strip of the pasta sheet in half lengthways, run your finger along the edge and then unfold. Repeat with the other sheet of pasta. Now place ½ teaspoon of the filling along the fold line, spacing 1¼ inches apart. Gently dab the top part of the fold with water using a pastry brush. Now take the bottom part of the sheet and fold over to the top edge. Gently pat between the filling and push around to remove any air pockets. Using a ravioli or pastry roller cutter, trim along the top of the sheet to give it a serrated edge, then roughly cut in between each filling to make the plin. Place the plin onto a floured tray. Repeat with the remaining pasta and filling.

Fill a 12-cup capacity saucepan with 6 cups of water, add some salt and bring to a boil. Heat a skillet (measuring 12½ inches in diameter by at least 2½ inches deep) over low heat. Add the plin to the boiling water and cook for 4½ minutes, then drain.

Meanwhile, add the butter and oil to the hot skillet, turn up the heat to medium and cook until the butter turns light brown. At this point, add the sage leaves and peas and cook for 1 minute.

Add the pasta cooking water and turn the heat down to low again. Add the drained plin, turn the heat back up to medium and toss the plin around in the butter sauce to coat. Divide among bowls with a little of the sauce spooned over. Top with the arugula and Parmesan. To add a little something extra to this dish, you could put a little of the pumpkin and yogurt purée (see page 239) under the plin.

Note It's a good idea to weigh egg yolks when making pasta for accuracy, especially if you're using free-range or organic eggs, as they vary in size.

1 *Roll the pasta out into sheets.*

2 *Place a heaping teaspoon of the pea and mascarpone filling on the fold line in the center of the pasta sheet, leaving about 1 inch between each dollop.*

3 *Brush the top edge of the pasta with water.*

4 *Fold the pasta over the filling.*

5 *Gently pat between the filling and push around to remove any air pockets.*

6 *Using a ravioli cutter trim along the top of the sheet to give it a serrated edge.*

SOME DIFFERENT BEANS AS A SALAD

SERVES 4

This is a variation of a garnish I used to do when I worked for Andrew McConnell.
It's now a home-meal regular. It has such a great contrast of texture and flavor.

2 SMALL RED ONIONS, SKIN ON

1 ½ CUPS GREEN BEANS, TOPS REMOVED

1 ½ CUPS YELLOW BEANS, TOPS REMOVED

13 OUNCES COOKED CANNELLINI
BEANS (SEE NOTE)

3 PLUM TOMATOES, QUARTERED, SEEDS
REMOVED AND FLESH CUT INTO THIN STRIPS

1 BUNCH BABY BASIL, OR 20 BASIL LEAVES,
FINELY CHOPPED

SEA SALT AND FRESHLY GROUND BLACK PEPPER

DRESSING

1 TABLESPOON DIJON MUSTARD

2 ⅔ OUNCES CRÈME FRAÎCHE

⅓ CUP EXTRA VIRGIN OLIVE OIL

2 TABLESPOONS CHARDONNAY VINEGAR

SEA SALT AND FRESHLY GROUND BLACK PEPPER

Preheat the oven to 400°F. Wrap the onions in foil and bake for 15–20 minutes or until a sharp knife pierces the onions easily. Take out of the oven, unwrap and set aside to cool.

Bring 4 cups of water to the boil with some salt. Add the green and yellow beans and cook for 4 minutes or until just still crisp. Drain and refresh in icy cold water. Drain again and place in a large bowl. Add the cannellini beans, tomato and basil. By this time the onions should be cool enough to peel off their outer skins. Cut the flesh into eighths and add to the beans. Season with salt and pepper.

For the dressing, whisk the mustard and crème fraîche together, then add the rest of the ingredients.

Pour the dressing over the bean mixture and serve. This salad is awesome for lunch the next day, too— just store in an airtight container in the fridge.

Note You can use 1 x 13 ounce can cooked cannellini beans, drained and rinsed, or 13 ounces cooked dried white beans. If using the latter, soak 7 ounces of dried white beans in plenty of water, then drain and cook in boiling water for 30 minutes or until tender.

Soak seeds in water for 24 hours before planting

THE FASTER IT GROWS THE
TASTIER & MORE TENDER IT WILL BE

RICH SOURCE OF
ANTIOXIDANTS & NUTRIENTS

It warms me to think of beet, their
beautiful color, earthiness and sweetness.

tolerates light frost

BEETS

BETALAIN

BEETS

Beets take close second place on the list of my favorite vegetables, just behind carrots. I do really love them. It warms me to think of them. Their bright beautiful color, the earthiness and sweetness they release simultaneously, the way they bleed all over your hands and stain your clothes. I just love them!

MY GRANDAD TOM'S PRIDE AND JOY

Beets are a veg I was brought up with. My Grandad Tom had them all through his garden, planted in between his roses, practically anywhere he could fit them in. I remember him pulling up humungous beets that he'd simply chop into quarters or roast whole and serve with a little bit of vinegar. Another of his favorite recipes was red beets and red cabbage pickle. He'd shred them both and transfer them into clean jars. Then he'd boil some malt vinegar, brown sugar, nutmeg and cinnamon to make a pickling liquid and pour it over the top of the grated veggies. He'd seal them up and store these jars of delight all over his house. I remember them in rows in his cupboards, and the pickles were a beautiful thing to eat.

GROWING

I've had great success over the years with growing beets, along with carrots and radishes, and they are a very satisfying plant to cultivate. I think this may have something to do with the fact that I find them so aesthetically pleasing. Even the beet seed itself is very beautiful—it almost looks like a clove.

They say you can hand sow all year round, but I've found in the height of summer the middle stalk of the beet tends to try and flower early, which transmits to the root and the beets will go quite woody. If you sow in late summer or autumn, they tend to do better as they are slower growing. But it's in spring they grow best. In spring they are just delicious.

VARIETIES

Growing your own has become a lot more interesting over the past few years because of all the different heritage (heirloom) varieties that have become available. There's Bull's Blood which is a deep red and Candy Stripe, which, as the name suggests, looks just like a lolly or sweet, with pink and white stripes. They are both so beautiful to look at. Then there are golden beets, which are becoming more common to the point where you can sometimes buy them in the big chain supermarkets. Another lovely heirloom variety is Cylindra, which is a longer, thinner style than the usual round beet. They add so much vibrant color to a dish.

I think the Candy Stripe or golds are best served raw to preserve their color. Just thinly slice or julienne them. However, if you have some lovely baby beets in red or gold, for a quick and easy pickle, boil them in water with wine, vinegar, salt and peppercorns added. For red beets, use red wine and red wine vinegar, and for golden beets, use white wine and white or chardonnay vinegar.

COOKING

The rule of thumb that I follow with cooking any vegetables is that if it grows below the ground (for example potatoes, beets or carrot), then start the vegetables in a pot with salted cold water—don't drop into already boiling water. This ensures they will cook evenly all the way through. Also you don't need to peel your beets prior to cooking. All you need to do to prepare them is remove all but about ½ inch of the stalk with a sharp knife and wash them thoroughly as they can hold quite a bit of grit in their stalks and leaves. Boil until tender (you should be able to insert and remove the tip of a knife easily into the beet), then leave them to sit in the cooking water for a few minutes until cooled slightly. Next, with gloved hands if you like, peel away the skin with your fingers. If they're cooked through, the skin should come away very easily and pretty much in one piece.

The great and frugal thing about beets is that you can use every bit of it. The stalk is beautiful sautéed. You can wash and use the small leaves in a salad and, for the larger ones, chop and wilt and use as you would spinach. In fact, when beets were first domesticated around the Mediterranean and Middle East, they were used mostly medicinally and as a dye. For many hundreds of years, it was only the leaves that were eaten until some bright spark decided to give the root a try.

Now it is a classic and much loved vegetable throughout most of the world, with the biggest beet-consuming regions being Britain, Scandinavia and Eastern Europe. Where would the Russians be without their national dish of borscht? It is such a beautiful, warming rosy soup. The beet's bold flavor goes wonderfully well with oily fish like kingfish or salmon and also fleshy fish like cod. It's just dynamite with meat and offal, and it can be the star of a dish all on its own. It particularly loves to be paired with the heat of horseradish or mustard leaf, which complements and enhances its natural sweetness. And it loves to act as a foil to the creamy richness of an earthy goat cheese or feta. All of these are classic flavor combinations, and my personal favorite is a slice of pickled beet on crusty white bread with a slice of cold ham.

Here's a little tip for you to avoid staining your chopping boards bright pink: wrap them in plastic wrap before grating or peeling your beets. When you're done, just remove the plastic and tip the mess straight into the garbage. Clever, hey?

BEETS, CELERY, APPLE & GINGER JUICE

MAKES 28 FLUID OUNCES, ENOUGH
FOR TWO NICE BIG GLASSES

*Being a bacon-and-egg-sandwich man in the morning, I have to say that this freshly juiced
beverage is bloody awesome alongside said sandwich. It awakens all the senses and vitalizes you
for the day ahead. Not that it happens regularly to me but it is also a great hangover cure.*

½ CUP CHOPPED FRESH GINGER

2 LARGE BEETS

4 SMALL STICKS CELERY

3 SMALL CARROTS

3 APPLES

10 ICE CUBES

The best thing about this recipe is that there is no peeling. Leave everything as is, just cut into sizes that fit the mouth of your electric juicer. Juice them down and pour the liquid into glasses filled with the ice. I do prefer it cold on ice but it isn't necessary. Drink straight away.

SALAD OF HEIRLOOM BEETS, SMOKED EEL, BRESAOLA, BLOOD ORANGE & BITTER LEAVES

→ *SERVES 4 AS AN ENTRÉE*

This is such a wonderful autumnal dish. The eels are at their height as they have fattened up throughout summer and stored their excess fat for the long cold winter. The contrast of the bitter leaves, earthiness of the beets and fresh citrussy acid of the blood orange leaves your palate coated with lots of wonderful flavors and textures. Freshly grated horseradish over the top is a great finishing touch.

2 BUNCHES HEIRLOOM BEETS
(GOLDEN, DETROIT, CANDY STRIPE
OR BULL'S BLOOD)

1 LARGE SMOKED EEL, SKINNED AND FILLETED

1 LARGE BLOOD ORANGE, SEGMENTED
AND JUICE RESERVED

⅔ CUP EXTRA VIRGIN OLIVE OIL

SEA SALT AND FRESHLY GROUND BLACK PEPPER

8 SLICES BRESAOLA (TRY TO GET WAGYU
AS IT ADDS A BEAUTIFUL FAT ELEMENT)

1 WHITE BELGIAN ENDIVE,
LEAVES PICKED

1 SMALL RED RADICCHIO, LEAVES PICKED AND TORN

1 YELLOW FRISÉE, HEART ONLY, LEAVES PICKED

3 TABLESPOONS CRÈME FRAÎCHE

2 TABLESPOONS SALTED BABY CAPERS, RINSED

Preheat the oven to 350°F.

Take 4 beets, wash the skin well and thinly slice on a mandoline. Place in a bowl of cold water until ready to serve.

Fill a 8-cup capacity saucepan with water, add some salt and the remaining beets, bring to a boil and cook for 7–11 minutes or until tender. Leave to cool in the cooking liquid.

Portion each fillet of smoked eel into 5 pieces and set aside on a baking sheet.

Whisk the blood orange juice and olive oil together in a bowl and season.

Once the beets have cooled, peel, cut in half and place in a large bowl. Add the bresaola, Belgian endive and radicchio. Add the frisée, blood orange segments and dress with a little of the dressing.

Put the tray of smoked eel into the oven and cook for 5 minutes.

Meanwhile, place a little crème fraîche in the center of each serving plate, arrange the cooked beet mixture on the plate, dollop over the rest of the crème fraîche and scatter over the capers. Drain the sliced raw beets and arrange on the plate. Add the smoked eel and drizzle over a little more dressing to serve.

FOIL-ROASTED BIG BEETS
WITH RICOTTA & MINT

SERVES 4 AS A SIDE

I love beets. This is just one of the many ways to enjoy it, simply done but so tasty.
We really should celebrate vegetables cooked without fuss much more.

4 BEETS, WASHED AND TRIMMED

OLIVE OIL, FOR DRIZZLING

SEA SALT AND FRESHLY GROUND BLACK PEPPER

1 GENEROUS TABLESPOON RED WINE VINEGAR

1 CUP FRESH RICOTTA, CRUMBLED

1 LARGE PINCH OF MINT LEAVES, TORN

Preheat the oven to 425°F.

Cut 2 sheets of foil and lay them across each other to make a cross. Put one beet in the middle, drizzle with olive oil, season with sale and pepper, then wrap up the beet to completely seal. Repeat with the remaining beets. Place on a baking sheet and roast for 1 hour. Insert a skewer through a bulbs to test to see if they're cooked.

Once done, carefully transfer onto a serving plate, unwrap, cut an "X" into the tops and push down like a jacket potato. Leave to cool for a few minutes.

Just before serving, drizzle over the vinegar, top with the ricotta and mint and season with a little more salt and pepper. I suggest scooping the beet flesh out without eating the skin.

SUSCEPTIBLE TO
APHIDS & CATERPILLARS OF
the CABBAGE WHITE BUTTERFLY

leave 16 inches between plants

GOOD COMPANION PLANTS

Dill
Sage
mint
beets
nasturtian
lettuce

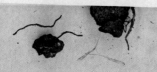

BROCCOLI

Traveled with the Romans
across the ancient world.

(*BRASSICA OLERACEA ITALICA*)

BROCCOLI

Broccoli is a member of the very large Brassica genus, which includes quite a few of my favorite vegetables such as cabbage, Brussels sprouts and cauliflower. All plants in the Brassica family are at their best through autumn, winter and spring. It also means they are quite slow growing. Broccoli, from planting to harvest, will take 3–4 months for a full head to ripen.

BROCCOLI LOVERS

Broccoli is native to Italy, where it has been cultivated since ancient Roman times. It was even mentioned in Apicius' book, one of the earliest surviving cookbooks, which gives us great insight into what the Romans ate and grew.

It came to England with the conquering Roman legions, who called it "broccolo," which translates as cabbage flower. The English at that time tended to call it "Italian asparagus," a quite misleading and confusing name, to be honest. Cabbage flower is actually much more apt and correct as broccoli and all the members of the *Brassica* genus originally descended from the cabbage. It was most likely selectively grown by farmers for its flowering head (kind of like an early form of genetic modification, if you will) and gradually became a species in its own right.

As it travelled with the Romans across the ancient world, broccoli became naturalized into many diets and cuisines. Asians love it and use the whole plant—trimming the woody outer layer from the stalk and slicing the sweet inner stem to use in stir-fries. They have also bred their own broccoli, called gai larn (otherwise known as Chinese broccoli).

Broccoli is at home in modern French cookery, and Italians love it, too, using it simply in classic dishes like orecchiette (little ear-shaped pasta) with chili, oil, bread crumbs and Parmesan. The flavor of the broccoli really shines through in this pasta dish. And the leaves themselves are lovely and sweet when sautéed.

VARIETIES

There are a few different varieties that are common now, but they are relatively new breeds like the Calabrese Sprouting and classic Albert (the one found in supermarkets). The Romanesco is another variety. It's very bizarre looking—it's quite pointy, looks like it's wearing a crown and is a lighter green color. It has a tighter head, which makes it look more like a cauliflower but it has a broccoli flavor. Then there are the modern hybrids like broccolini, which has been bred for its long, fine stalks, and broccoflower, which as the name suggests is a cross between broccoli and cauliflower.

COOKING

When you are cooking your broccoli, or anything green for that matter, be aware that when it loses its beautiful vibrant color and begins to turn dark, this means it is starting to lose its nutrients. This is a shame for a plant like broccoli, as it is rich in vitamin A, lots of different vitamin Bs and even contains a good amount of vitamin C. Then there are the good minerals it carries like folic acid, calcium, manganese and zinc. To retain as many of the vitamins in the broccoli as possible (and avoid them leaching out into the cooking water for you only to chuck down the sink), cut your broc into small florets. This will reduce the cooking time also. You could even try it raw—in a similar fashion to the cauliflower salad recipe on page 96. Like most vegetables, broccoli should be served *al dente*, not mushy, and it should have a nice mouthfeel and bite to it.

GROWING

If you are going to have a go at growing your own lovely broccoli, then just remember, being a *Brassica*, don't attempt to grow broccoli through summer: if you do, it will bolt and flower before it has produced a proper head, and you will get spindly florets instead. Stick to autumn, winter and spring crops.

The *Brassica* genus as a whole is susceptible to various pests. And broccoli will most definitely attract white fly and cabbage moth. A pyrethrum spray will get rid of these pests, but if you want a natural deterrent in the form of a companion plant, then put in some thyme or rosemary. Their strong fragrance will deter the cabbage moth. Dill is also a good companion as it will attract predator wasps that eat the moths. However, if you don't want to encourage wasps into your garden, stick with the stronger smelling herbs instead.

Broccoli is a frost-hardy plant once established, but not as a young seedling, so if you know there is going to be a frost, it's wise to make a frost cover to protect your babies. Just take a 8-cup capacity milk bottle and cut it widthways at the top of the label and place the cover over your seedlings. It will not only protect them against frost but it will also stop slugs and snails getting in.

Another way to protect the seedlings is to plant them close together. Once they have established themselves, you need to keep a lookout for any sign of flowering. The minute you see a flower, clip it—this will prevent the plant from going to seed and help produce a tighter head of broccoli.

LINGUINI OF BROCCOLI, HERBS & HAZELNUT CRUMB

SERVES 2 (GREAT WHEN YOU
GET HOME AND ARE IN A RUSH)

*If you've never tried this quick and simple dish at home before,
well, this may just become your new best friend.*

HAZELNUT CRUMB

¼ CUP HAZELNUTS

1 ¾ OUNCES CIABATTA BREAD (CRUSTS ON),
TORN INTO PINKY-FINGERNAIL-SIZED PIECES

2 TEASPOONS THYME LEAVES

6 ¾ OUNCES DRIED LINGUINI

2 TABLESPOONS BUTTER

1 GENEROUS TABLESPOON OLIVE OIL

¾ CUP PANCETTA, DICED (OPTIONAL)

1 LARGE SHALLOT, SLICED

1 GARLIC CLOVE, THINLY SLICED

½ LONG RED CHILI, THINLY SLICED

6 ANCHOVY FILLETS

1 HEAD OF BROCCOLI FLORETS
AND STALK, CHOPPED

3 TABLESPOONS PASTA COOKING WATER

3 TABLESPOONS WHITE WINE

8 LARGE BASIL LEAVES, FINELY CHOPPED

¼ BUNCH ITALIAN PARSLEY, LEAVES
PICKED AND CHOPPED

JUICE OF 1 LEMON

10 TURNS OF BLACK PEPPER FROM A MILL

FINELY GRATED PARMESAN, TO SERVE

For the hazelnut crumb, preheat the oven to 350°F. Roast the hazelnuts for 5–10 minutes. Place in a tea towel and rub off the skins while still warm. Roughly chop and place in a large bowl. Set aside.

Turn up the oven to 400°F. Place the bread on a baking sheet and bake for 3–5 minutes or until dried and crispy. Add to the hazelnuts, along with the thyme.

Bring 8 cups of salted water to the boil. Add the linguine and cook for 6–7 minutes or until *al dente*. Take off the heat and allow the pasta to sit in the water.

Meanwhile, place a large skillet over medium heat, add the butter, olive oil and pancetta and cook until the pancetta softens. Add the shallot, garlic and chili, turn down the heat to low and cook until softened. Turn the heat up to medium, add the anchovies and broccoli and cook, stirring frequently, for 4 minutes. Add the pasta cooking water and wine, turn up the heat to high and reduce the liquid to one-quarter. Drain the pasta and add to the sauce. Stir to incorporate all the ingredients. Take off the heat and add the herbs, lemon juice and pepper. Divide among bowls and scatter over the Parmesan and hazelnut crumb (see Note).

Note Any left-over hazelnut crumb can be kept in an airtight container in the cupboard area for up to 3 months—I've always a little up my sleeve just in case I think a dish may need it.

BROCCOLI, CAPER & RAISIN DRESSING

→ SERVES 4–6

Not only does this dressing go well with broccoli, but it's also great with a simple piece of broiled steak. Try it out with other vegetables and fish too. You'll be amazed by how much you will fall in love with this dressing. It's the new-age pesto. It keeps for days on end in the fridge, just as long as it is submerged under olive oil.

2 SMALL HEADS OF BROCCOLI

SEA SALT

CAPER & RAISIN DRESSING

1 TABLESPOON SALTED BABY CAPERS, RINSED

1 TABLESPOON RAISINS, SOAKED FOR
5 MINUTES IN WARM WATER, THEN DRAINED

3 ANCHOVY FILLETS

1 RED BIRD'S EYE CHILI, HALVED,
SEEDS REMOVED AND CHOPPED

1 GARLIC CLOVE, CRUSHED

5 BASIL LEAVES

2 TEASPOONS BALSAMIC VINEGAR

JUICE OF ½ LEMON

⅓ CUP EXTRA VIRGIN OLIVE OIL

SEA SALT AND FRESHLY GROUND BLACK PEPPER

For the caper and raisin dressing, add all the solid ingredients to a large mortar and pound to a sticky paste consistency. Add all the liquid ingredients and taste for seasoning. Add salt and pepper if needed but remember the anchovies and capers are naturally salty. Set aside.

To prepare the broccoli, first peel the stem. I love broccoli stem so don't throw this out. Peel the stem, then cut each floret so that it has some stem attached. (Discard the core of the stem.) By the end you should have what looks like hand-cut broccolini with the exception of a few florets and bits.

Bring 4 cups of water to the boil with some salt. Add the broccoli and cook for 3 minutes, then drain. Place in a bowl and add enough of the dressing to heavily coat the broccoli. Serve straight away.

BROCCOLINI & GRAINS

SERVES 4

This dish is delicious with some steamed chunky white-fleshed fish or a roasted lobster tail (if you're flush or have just caught your own). You can use any type of whole grains but I recommend the ones below to achieve the correct texture and nuttiness for this dish.

2 POUNDS 4 OUNCES CLAMS, SOAKED IN WATER FOR 20 MINUTES, THEN THOROUGHLY RINSED AND DRAINED

1 ¼ CUPS WHITE WINE

1 CUP COOKED QUINOA (SEE PAGE 276)

1 CUP COOKED PEARL BARLEY (SEE PAGE 276)

½ CUP COOKED SPELT GRAIN (SEE PAGE 276)

½ CUP COOKED FREGOLA (SEE PAGE 276)

1 BUNCH BROCCOLINI, CHOPPED

2 TABLESPOONS MASCARPONE

½ CUP FINELY GRATED PARMESAN

2 TABLESPOONS CHOPPED SORREL

2 TABLESPOONS CHOPPED ITALIAN PARSLEY

6 BASIL LEAVES, CHOPPED

FINE SEA SALT AND FRESHLY GROUND BLACK PEPPER

Place a saucepan (measuring about 10 ½ inches in diameter by 4¼ inches deep) over high heat. Once hot, add the clams, then the wine. Cover with a tight-fitting lid and cook for 5–7 minutes or until the clams have opened. Pass through a fine strainer, reserving both the clams and the juices. Pick the clam meat from the shells.

Wash the pan, then place all the grains in it. Add enough of the reserved clam cooking juices to cover the grains by ⅝ inch. If there isn't enough liquid, add some water. Bring to a boil, add the broccolini and clam meat, turn down to medium heat and cook. Once the broccolini is tender, fold in the mascarpone, Parmesan and herbs. Season with salt and pepper and serve.

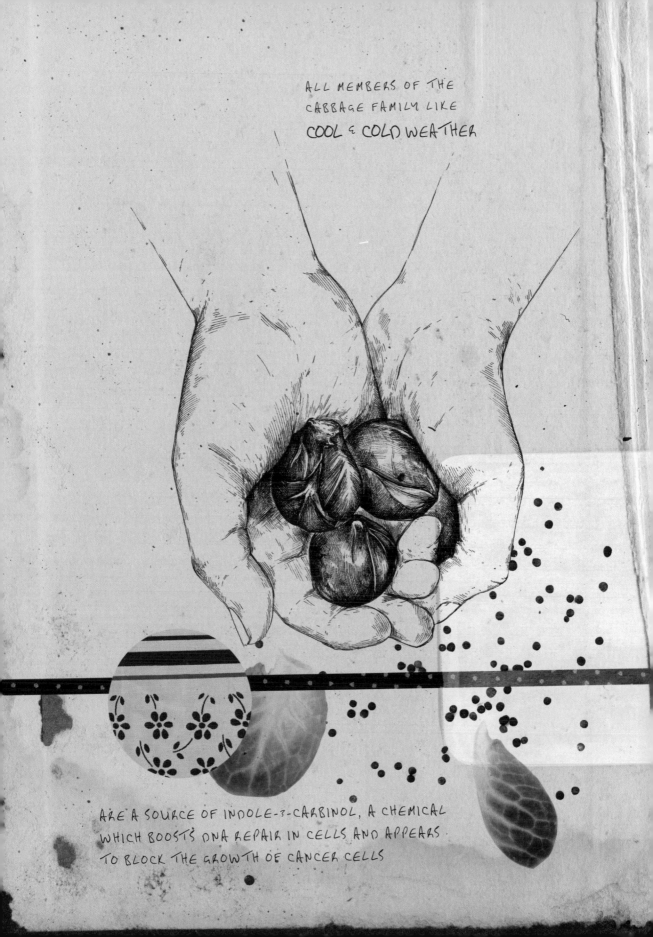

ALL MEMBERS OF THE
CABBAGE FAMILY LIKE
COOL & COLD WEATHER

ARE A SOURCE OF INDOLE-3-CARBINOL, A CHEMICAL
WHICH BOOSTS DNA REPAIR IN CELLS AND APPEARS
TO BLOCK THE GROWTH OF CANCER CELLS

Part of the Brassica family Brussels sprouts are closely related to cabbage, broccoli, cauliflower and kale. Out of all their cousins sprouts have the worst reputation. Wholly undeserved, in my opinion.

BRUSSELS SPROUTS

EXCELLENT SOURCE OF VITAMINS

BRUSSELS SPROUTS

(BRASSICA OLERACEA GEMMIFERA)

If you have ever seen a Brussels sprout plant growing you would undoubtedly think it was the ugliest, wartiest looking specimen you've ever seen, and not something at all edible. You look at its bizarre trunk with countless little green knobs growing from it and think, "God, what is that? It's a cabbage gone wrong!" And, well, it is.

WHAT'S IN A NAME?

So why Brussels sprouts? Well, the obvious answer seems to be "because that's where they came from," but there isn't a lot of evidence to support that statement, although they are popular in Belgium. They probably did originate in Europe and, much like most things, the Romans spread them throughout the continent.

They are a cultivar, or cultivated variety, of the cabbage, which means they were grown and bred from the cabbage specifically for their smaller heads until they became a sub-species in their own right. So there you go. There's no need to be afraid of the Brussels sprout—they're just a mini cabbage.

A MUCH MALIGNED VEG

Brussels sprouts are part of the *Brassica* family and closely related to cabbage, broccoli, cauliflower, kohlrabi and kale. It's a real "love it" or "hate it" veg, and, out of all its cousins, poor sprouts probably have the worst reputation. And a wholly undeserved one, in my opinion.

It is a beautiful delicate little vegetable, and I have always loved it. I remember Sunday dinner at my nan's when I was younger (a weekly occurrence) and my sister Lucy getting in trouble every week for getting up from her chair to move the platter of sprouts further away from her. She couldn't even stand to be near them! I didn't mind, as long as she moved them closer to me. I think I'd have a dozen for every one Mum made Lucy eat. And my fondness for them has only grown with the ensuing years, as I've learned that treating them with a little love and respect will reward you again and again.

COOKING

I actually do blame the moms, dads, pops and nans of this world for completely cooking the life out of Brussels sprouts, bastardizing them so that the entire house smells, well, there really is no delicate way to put this, it smells like farts. My nan was one of the guilty parties, believe me. It didn't put me off sprouts, though, but I will readily admit that she would boil them on high heat for at least an hour before serving so that they resembled waterlogged gray walnuts, with not a single thing gorgeous or green left about them. Certainly, they didn't retain any of the vitamins or minerals that sprouts are naturally endowed with—these would have all gone down the drain. In fact, these little beauties are vitamin powerhouses, they're high in protein and anti-oxidants and can be described with all those other buzzwords that equal "good for you." But that is only if they are cooked correctly. So let me tell you how, and believe me, it is this simple …

Never, never, never cook them all the way through. Cook them until just *al dente*—that is, still with a little bite to them, then take them off the heat immediately as they will carry on cooking. By the time you dress them, either with a little olive oil or butter and some salt and pepper, and get them on the table, they will be just perfect for eating.

Their flavor is so delicate and sweet, yet so robust. They make a classic accompaniment when paired with chestnuts, thyme, mint and bacon.

There are a few other ways I like to cook them for a good result. You can finely chop the sprouts and cook them in lightly salted boiling water. Meanwhile, heat some butter until foaming and toss the drained sprouts through. Season and eat straight away. Cutting them finely reduces the cooking time.

I also enjoy peeling the individual leaves from the head. Discard any discolored or straggly outer ones and use the lovely tender inner leaves. Just lightly blanch them in boiling water and refresh under cold water. This will take away the "plasticky" coating on the outside of the leaves but they will retain their lovely raw, crunchy texture, much like cabbage. This is one of my favorite sides.

GROWING

As I mentioned, the Brussels sprout plant is a weird-looking one, but strangely beautiful in its own way. It is also really great to grow, and ideally suited for small spaces as it grows straight up. It will take quite some time to mature, about 3–6 months, like most members of the Brassica family, but you should enjoy a yield of about 2 pounds 4 ounces of sprouts per plant.

MASHED BRUSSELS SPROUTS WITH MINT, BEST END OF LAMB

→ SERVES 4

This is the clincher. If you have been in the "don't go near Brussels sprouts" school then this will convert you. I personally love them, and this is my fail-safe recipe to cooking them well—the mint and vinegar help soften the flavor of the sprouts and I couldn't think of anything better to serve them with than a roasted best end of lamb.

2 POUNDS 4 OUNCES–2 POUNDS 10 OUNCES BEST END OF LAMB (SEE NOTE)

OLIVE OIL, FOR SEARING

12 BRUSSELS SPROUTS

1 GENEROUS TABLESPOON OLIVE OIL

1 GENEROUS TABLESPOON CHARDONNAY VINEGAR

1 BIG PINCH OF MINT LEAVES, THINLY SLICED

FINE SEA SALT AND FRESHLY GROUND BLACK PEPPER

Preheat the oven to 425°F. Heat the olive oil in a large skillet over high heat for 1 minute. Sear the lamb on all sides until a nice caramelized brown color, about 4 minutes all up, then transfer to a roasting tray and place in the oven for 35–45 minutes. Remove from the oven and allow to rest, then carve into slices to serve.

Meanwhile, trim the bases of the Brussels sprouts, peel off the outer dark green leaves and quarter. Place the sprouts in a 8-cup capacity saucepan, cover with water and bring to a boil, then turn down to a simmer and cook for 10–13 minutes. Immediately drain, then add the sprouts back to the pan and place over low heat. You want to dry the sprouts out a little for 1–2 minutes. Take off the heat and mash roughly 8–10 times with an old-school hand-held masher. Now stir in the olive oil, vinegar and mint, season with salt and pepper and serve with the lamb.

Note Best of lamb is an old English cut of meat. It's the best part of the neck and shoulder with 4 racks (or points) attached.

ROASTED BRUSSELS SPROUTS, VANILLA-CONFIT CHESTNUTS & THYME

SERVES 4 AS A SIDE

Remember that Brussels sprouts are delicious until they're overcooked.
Then they emanate a farty smell and will taste like how the grans of the past cooked them.
Follow this recipe to the "T" and I assure you that you will love the Brussels.

7 OUNCES SWEET CHESTNUTS	SEA SALT AND FRESHLY GROUND BLACK PEPPER
¾ CUP VANILLA SYRUP (SEE PAGE 143)	2 TABLESPOONS BUTTER, DICED
20-30 BRUSSELS SPROUTS	5 SPRIGS THYME, LEAVES PICKED AND FINELY CHOPPED
3 TABLESPOONS OLIVE OIL	

Preheat the oven to 425°F. Score the top of the chestnuts with a sharp knife, place on a baking sheet and bake for 5 minutes or until they start to split open at the cut. Cool slightly, then peel while still warm.

Turn down the oven to 400°F. Place the peeled chestnuts and vanilla syrup in a small saucepan (4 inches in diameter) and bring to a boil, then turn down the heat to low and simmer for 15–17 minutes. Set aside.

Trim the bases of the Brussels sprouts, peel off the outer dark green leaves and halve. (You can either throw the outer leaves away or have a go at making the salad of Brussels sprout leaves, mozzarella, white anchovies on page 52). Heat a large skillet over high heat. Add the olive oil and warm for 1 minute, then add the sprouts, cut side down, and sauté for 4 minutes. Drain the chestnuts from the syrup with a slotted spoon and add to the pan. (Discard the syrup or save to use again.) Season with salt and pepper, add the butter and thyme and once the butter has melted, give it a good stir. Pour into a large ovenproof serving dish and roast for 12–15 minutes. Serve straight away.

SALAD OF BRUSSELS SPROUT LEAVES, MOZZARELLA, WHITE ANCHOVIES

*SERVES 2 AS AN ENTRÉE
OR AS A SIDE SALAD TO SHARE*

You just wouldn't know how delicious Brussels sprouts leaves in a salad are until you actually eat them in this way. This recipe can be adapted—use all sorts of delicious things you like.

2 TABLESPOONS WALNUTS

4 ⅓ OUNCES BRUSSELS SPROUT LEAVES (THE OUTER LEAVES, NOT THE INNER TOUGHER ONES)

½ CUP PICKED WATERCRESS

1 TEASPOON HONEY

1 ½ TABLESPOONS RED WINE VINEGAR

3 TABLESPOONS EXTRA VIRGIN OLIVE OIL

2 TABLESPOONS CURRANTS, SOAKED IN WARM WATER FOR 5 MINUTES, THEN DRAINED

8–12 WHITE ANCHOVY FILLETS

2 SHALLOTS, THINLY SLICED

1 SMALL (ABOUT 4 OUNCE) BUFFALO MOZZARELLA BALL, CUT INTO 8 SLICES

6 BASIL LEAVES, TORN

2 TABLESPOONS FINELY CHOPPED ITALIAN PARSLEY

SEA SALT AND FRESHLY GROUND BLACK PEPPER

CRUSTY FRENCH BAGUETTE, TORN, TO SERVE

Preheat the oven to 350°F. Place the walnuts on a baking sheet and roast for 3–5 minutes or until fragrant. Allow to cool slightly, then roughly chop and set aside.

Bring a saucepan of salted water to the boil. Add the sprout leaves, allow to come back to the boil and cook for 1 minute. Drain, then refresh under cold water. Pat the leaves dry and place in a large bowl with the watercress.

Place the honey in a small saucepan over low heat, add the vinegar, bring to a boil, then add the olive oil and take off the heat. Stir in the currants and walnuts and set aside. This is the dressing for the whole dish.

Add the anchovies and shallots to the sprout leaves and dress with a little of the dressing. Place the mozzarella onto plates, arrange the sprout mixture around the mozzarella, dress with a little more of the dressing, then scatter over the herbs. Finish with salt and pepper. Serve with the bread to mop the dressing up with.

IS A HERBACEOUS, BIENNIAL, DICOTYLECONOUS FLOWERING PLANT

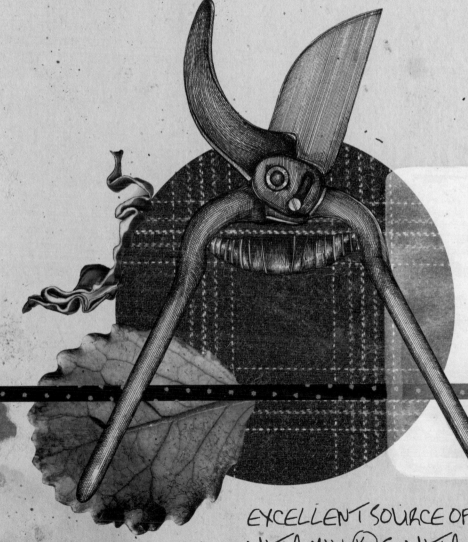

EXCELLENT SOURCE OF VITAMIN Ⓚ & VITAMIN Ⓒ

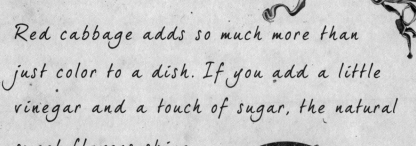

Red cabbage adds so much more than just color to a dish. If you add a little vinegar and a touch of sugar, the natural sweet flavors shine.

CABBAGE

all members of the cabbage family like cool and even cold weather.

CABBAGE

Can't stomach plain old white cabbage, because of the memories of the smell, off-putting color or texture of all the bad cabbage you have eaten before? Then it is time to put those prejudices aside and begin again. Just like its fair cousin the Brussels sprout, cabbage gets a bad rap when it truly is a delightful and delicate vegetable that is crying out to be respected and treated well.

CABBAGE PATCH KID

Oh, cabbage. My first memory of cabbage is the short drive from Barnsley, in the UK, where we lived, to Darfield, where my aunty lived, every Sunday for lunch—Dad driving, Mum in the front and my elder sister, Lucy, and I in the back seat. We would pass a huge field on the left-hand side planted with cabbage and every time, without fail, Lucy would look over at that field, then lean in and whisper in my ear, "We found you in a box in that cabbage patch." For years I actually thought my parents did find me in a cabbage patch! It used to upset me no end. Kids can be so cruel.

SAUERKRAUT TO SLAW

My Grandad Tom used to grow massive cabbages in his back garden, and it is a very popular and traditional English thing to find people cultivating cabbage in their allotments, which are small parcels of land that people lease from the local councils and they must be specifically used for growing food. They were introduced about 1,000 years ago, originally to compensate farmers who were forced from their lands by invasions and conquests, allowing them a subsistence living. Allotments today are hugely popular among people living in denser cities with no room for their own gardens. And in just about every single one, you will find cabbage growing. Perhaps this is a throwback to the time when growing your own food was really a matter of survival.

When you really look at it, cabbage is a staple of poorer economies the whole world over, and it plays a huge part in their national cuisine, particularly in the Eastern European bloc, where it is a cheap way to bulk out food. The Polish have their beautiful little traditional parcels of pierogi. The Germans ferment their cabbage and turn it into their famous Sauerkraut. And let's not forget the cabbage leaves stuffed with ground meat and rice or barley held so dear by Czechs, Poles, Slovaks and Serbs alike. Cabbage abounds as beautiful, warm comfort food everywhere. Personally, coleslaw has my heart. I just love it. I can't get enough of it.

There are so many varieties of cabbage, and different methods of serving it. As with Brussels sprouts, don't let the fact that older generations absolutely abused this gorgeous vegetable put you off using it.

WHITE CABBAGE

Don't overlook white cabbage, or the finer Savoy. Just slice it as thin as you possibly can to reduce the cooking time. And if you reduce the cooking time, you will also reduce the amount of nutrients that you lose. I mean, by the time our nans had let the cabbage stew for three hours, besides being able to smell it from four doors away, nutritionally there was simply no point in eating it. All those lovely vitamins have gone down the sink with the cooking water. Simple braised cabbage is so easy, and just delicious. Just cook it quickly over high heat mixed with oil and butter and, as the juices leach out, add a dash of white wine or water. This will boil immediately and steam the cabbage at the same time as it's sautéing in the pan. In about a minute, you will have a perfect side for a nice piece of pork.

RED CABBAGE

But then there is red cabbage, which adds so much more than just eye-catching color to a dish. If you add a little bit of vinegar (a nice red wine or raspberry vinegar would be perfect for this type) and just a touch of sugar, the natural sweet flavors and moisture are drawn from the cabbage and really serve to lift the whole dish. Red cabbage is also amazing to pickle and preserve. You will get vast amounts even from one head of cabbage. I find that the nicest, sweetest leaves

are just under the outer leaves that you need to peel back and remove. Once you get further in towards the center, the leaves tend to be woody, and I find these better for pickling.

TUSCAN CABBAGE

And if you want something different, that will add beauty to your garden as well as your plate, go for Tuscan cabbage. This goes by a number of different names, including black cabbage, black kale and cavolo nero. It is all one and the same and just lovely. Treat it as you would Swiss chard. Shred it and eat it raw, the Italian way (it's a revelation!), sauté it in a pan or add to a soup or braise in the last few minutes to wilt the leaves to add wonderful color and texture. The curly dark leaves are a gorgeous ornamental addition to your garden bed and are so easy to grow and use.

GROWING

In fact, cabbage is fairly easy to grow in general. They do well in most soil, don't need a lot of water and don't mind a bit of cold or frost. The only down side is white cabbage is a large plant. It therefore requires a bit of space to produce a good head and they will take six months to mature from seed. So, if this is an issue for you, look to the Tuscan variety, which is much more compact and faster growing.

TRUFFLED COLESLAW
WITH GOLDEN SPICED QUAIL KIEV

SERVES 4

Who doesn't love chicken kiev? It's a pub standard. I've used quail—a small chicken, really—but you can adapt this recipe and use chicken in exactly the same way. This dish comes with a warning: don't wear your best dress or bow tie. Let the cooked quails cool a little because when you bite into them they have a tendency to shoot out their butter filling all over the place. (This may seem fun if you see it happen, but not fun when it gets you in the eye or on your nicest neighbor ever, who turns on his/her heels and leaves, then presents you with their dry-cleaning bill the next day ... then proceeds to tell you that your fence is actually on their side of the plot. Believe me, this happens.)

This dish is great for kids and adults alike. The recipe is easier than it looks, I swear. It is all about the stages of preparation. Please remember to read through the recipe and ingredients to make sure you have everything prepared.

GARLIC BUTTER

1 CUP UNSALTED BUTTER, SOFTENED

3 ½ OUNCES GARLIC, MINCED

6 BASIL LEAVES, CHOPPED

¼ BUNCH ITALIAN PARSLEY, LEAVES PICKED AND CHOPPED

FINE SEA SALT AND FRESHLY GROUND BLACK PEPPER

SPICED QUAILS

4 JUMBO QUAILS

2 TABLESPOONS CORIANDER SEEDS

1 ½ TABLESPOONS CUMIN SEEDS

1 ½ TABLESPOONS WHITE PEPPERCORNS

2 TEASPOONS MUSTARD SEEDS

2 TEASPOONS GROUND TURMERIC

2 TABLESPOONS GROUND GINGER

1 TABLESPOON SEA SALT

1 CUP ALL-PURPOSE FLOUR OR RICE FLOUR

1 ⅔ CUPS BUTTERMILK

TRUFFLED COLESLAW

¼ RED CABBAGE, FINELY SHREDDED

¼ SAVOY CABBAGE, FINELY SHREDDED

FINE SEA SALT AND FRESHLY GROUND BLACK PEPPER

1 SMALL CARROT, THINLY SLICED, THEN CUT INTO THIN STRIPS

½ LARGE RED ONION, THINLY SLICED

1 CUP MAYONNAISE

⅓ CUP TRUFFLE OIL

VEGETABLE OIL, FOR DEEP-FRYING

For the garlic butter, place all the ingredients in a mixing bowl and whip with a handheld beater until fully incorporated. Transfer to a piping (frosting) bag fitted with a small plain nozzle (about the size of a pea) and set aside at room temperature until ready to use.

For the spiced quails, debone each bird into breasts and legs (or if you and your butcher are close, I'm sure they'll do it for you). For the breast pieces, remove the last two joints of the wings and French the remaining wing bone. Make a small insertion, using a small sharp knife, into the breast meat next to the wing but go as deep as you can—the more room the more butter you will be able to fit in. Pipe the garlic butter into the incision of each quail breast. Place the pieces of quail on a tray and refrigerate to firm up the butter.

For the leg pieces, remove the thigh bone leaving the leg bone intact. Pipe the butter into the leg bone cavity, fold over the meat on each side to enclose the butter and refrigerate to firm up the butter.

Gently toast all the spices in a dry skillet over low heat for about 4 minutes to release the natural oils. Place in a mortar and grind until the consistency of ground black pepper. Tip into a fairly large bowl, add the salt and flour and stir to combine. Place the buttermilk in another bowl. Take a piece of quail and dip it into the buttermilk, then into the spiced flour. Repeat this process again and place the piece of quail on a tray. Crumb the remaining pieces of quail. Place in the fridge until ready to cook.

For the truffled coleslaw, place both cabbages in a bowl, lightly salt and set aside for 5 minutes. Rinse the cabbage, then dry on a tea towel. Place in a large bowl, add the remaining ingredients and mix well. Set aside.

Preheat the oven to 375°F. If you have a deep-fryer, heat 6 cups of vegetable oil to 340°F and deep-fry the breast and leg pieces for 2 minutes or until nice and golden, then place in a roasting tray and finish cooking in the oven for 5 minutes. If you don't have a deep-fryer, never mind, help is at hand. Pour 2 cups of vegetable oil into a deep saucepan (but not more than one-third full) over medium heat and heat to 340°F. Add the quail pieces and fry until nice and golden, then place in a roasting tray and finish cooking in the oven for 8 minutes. Serve straight away with some coleslaw on the side.

1 *Prepare the garlic butter and debone the quail into breasts and legs.*

2 *Using a sharp knife, make a small, deep insertion into the breast meat next to the wing. For the leg pieces, remove the thigh bone but leave the bone intact.*

3 *Pipe the garlic butter into the breast cavity.*

4 *Continue to pipe the garlic butter into each of the quail pieces.*

5 *Dip quail pieces into buttermilk.*

6 *Coat each quail piece in spiced flour.*

SAUTÉED TUSCAN CABBAGE
& MATSUTAKE MUSHROOM PASTA

SERVES 4

This beautifully flavored and textured Tuscan cabbage sits stunningly with the wild flavored matsutake mushrooms. It's one of my favorite autumnal dishes, enjoyed in front of the fire with a glass of red wine. But it does go well with a cheeky cider too.

14 OUNCES CRESTE DI GALLO PASTA (SEE NOTE) OR ANY THICK PASTA SHAPE

⅓ CUP OLIVE OIL

1 BUNCH TUSCAN CABBAGE (CAVOLO NERO), STALKS REMOVED, SHREDDED

10 ½ OUNCES MATSUTAKE MUSHROOMS, OR SAFFRON MILK CAPS, BRUSHED AND THICKLY SLICED

2 SHALLOTS, THINLY SLICED

2 GARLIC CLOVES, SLICED

3 ½ TABLESPOONS BUTTER, DICED

¾ CUP PASTA COOKING WATER

3 TABLESPOONS CHOPPED ITALIAN PARSLEY

JUICE OF 1 LEMON

SEA SALT AND FRESHLY GROUND BLACK PEPPER

FINELY GRATED PARMESAN, TO SERVE

Bring 6 cups of salted water to the boil. Add the pasta and cook for 7–9 minutes or until *al dente*. Take off the heat and allow the pasta to sit in the water.

Meanwhile, heat the olive oil in a large skillet over medium heat. Add the Tuscan cabbage and sauté until tender. Add the mushrooms, shallots, garlic and butter, turn down the heat and cook out for 4–5 minutes. Turn up the heat, add the pasta cooking water and stir to make an emulsion of sorts. Drain the pasta and add to the pan. Add the parsley and lemon juice, season with salt and pepper and divide among bowls. Finish with the grated Parmesan.

Note Creste di gallo pasta resembles the cockscomb on a chicken, hence its Italian name that means "chicken's crown." It is great for ragù-style pasta sauces as it soaks up the juices and adds texture to hearty dishes.

SIMPLE BRAISED RED CABBAGE WITH CUMBERLAND SAUSAGES

SERVES 4

This may just be one of the first recipes I ever made when working for Mike Taylor at Warren House just outside of London. My version here has been altered and played with but the base recipe came from one of the English queens of cookery Delia Smith. It's just so simple and beautiful with all sorts of meat but who could go past the great English sausage, the Cumberland. (Although wherever you are from in England, you probably think your sausage is the best, especially if you're from Lincolnshire.)

1 STAR ANISE

1 JUNIPER BERRY

1 WHOLE CLOVE

1 CARDAMOM POD

½ CUP UNREFINED LIGHT BROWN SUGAR

½ SMALL RED CABBAGE, FINELY SHREDDED

2 LARGE WHITE ONIONS, SLICED

4 COOKING APPLES (SEE NOTES), PEELED AND DICED

⅓ CUP RED WINE VINEGAR

3 ½ TABLESPOONS BUTTER, DICED

SEA SALT AND FRESHLY GROUND BLACK PEPPER

4-8 CUMBERLAND SAUSAGES (SEE NOTES)

VEGETABLE OIL, FOR DRIZZLING

WHITE BREAD, TO SERVE

Ground the spices and sugar together using a mortar and pestle. Place the spice mixture, cabbage, onion, apple, vinegar and butter in a large saucepan over medium heat, season with salt and pepper and cook, stirring occasionally, for 45–60 minutes or until completely softened and moist.

Preheat the oven to 400°F. Place the sausages in a roasting tray, drizzle over some vegetable oil and roast for 12 minutes or until cooked.

Spoon the cabbage mixture into a large serving dish and top with the sausages. A few slices of good old white bread works wonders with this.

Notes I like to use Pippins for cooking with. Use a sharp non-cooking apple if these varieties aren't available.

The size of Cumberland sausages varies from butcher to butcher. You should find them at your local butcher.

PEPPERS ARE A GENUS
OF FLOWERING PLANTS
IN THE NIGHTSHADE FAMILY

Peppers are a lovely plant to grow.
When I moved to London I used to
grow them on my windowsill to add
color. They are perfect for a
windowbox and like plenty of sun

Native to the Americas, where they have been cultivated for thousands of years.

VITAMIN C

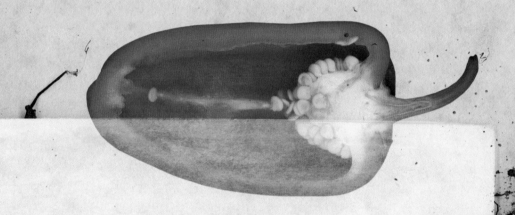

PEPPERS

ARE MOSTLY PERENNIALS.
BUT ARE GENERALLY
TREATED AS ANNUALS

PEPPERS

Peppers are a very lovely decorative plant with such vibrant color. The pepper (or capsicum) is a very close relative to the chili and comes in a rainbow of colors: red, green, orange, yellow and even purple. They originated in the Americas, where good old Chris Columbus picked them up and brought them back to Spain, where they were heartily embraced. Except by me.

OVERUSED AND ABUSED

I am going to go straight ahead and say for the record I hate peppers, raw or cooked. Hell to me would be a final meal of roasted peppers. The first thought that crosses my mind is "World's Worst Food," not something I'm partial to having included in *Mr. Wilkinson's Vegetables*. It was only under the editorial guidance from my publisher that I began to consider including peppers. Mainly because so many people out there love it. So, I went away and thought about this, and then, after reflecting on it, I realized just how many recipes I did have for peppers—either in a sauce or as an accompaniment. There were at least 20, which I have shortlisted down to the three in this chapter.

I think my initial hesitation is because they just weren't in my cultural repertoire growing up. My family never used them. And then, in the mid-nineties, thanks to the likes of River Café and Antonio Carluccio, there was a renaissance, an embracing of Italian food in England, with eggplant, fennel and peppers appearing on just about every menu. They was overused at the time, and that is probably why I have habitually steered away from them. They are nice in a traditional dish like ratatouille, but then again I have had some seriously bad ratatouille in my time, and it also seemed that if you walked into any British pub, the side salad would consist of grated carrot, iceberg lettuce, a slice of cucumber and diced green peppers, which (I'm sorry to say) is disgusting no matter what you do with it. It just seems like peppers, when prepared badly and without care, can be their own worst enemy: bitter seeds, indigestible skin.

PREPARING AND COOKING

Thankfully, there are some things you can do to make peppers much more attractive and palatable, and these are really very simple. Roasting or charring and peeling away the skin removes some of the bitter flavor and toughness. Also discard the seeds, and just use the lovely flesh. Just by exposing the flesh to heat, it becomes softer and releases its natural oils, which is where a lot of the flavor lies. There are also some amazing preserved varieties you can pick up. Of these, I like using piquillo peppers, which are small, sweet and slightly spicy peppers from Spain. They are already pre-roasted and peeled, making life very easy indeed. You should be able to find them at any good deli.

GROWING

Having just explained my dislike of peppers, they are, in fact, a really lovely plant to grow, but they weren't something that I inherited a passion for from Dad and Grandad, as with the many other things I like to grow. It was when I moved to London in 1996 for work that I began to grow them on my windowsill to add a little color to the place. I never really used them but would give them to friends. I just liked to grow them. They can tolerate a small space if they have enough sun, making them perfect for a window box or even just inside the window on the sill.

In more recent times, I have been particularly successful in growing peppers—it seems not too many critters like to nip at them except the little red spider. To achieve full ripeness through summer, planting earlier in cooler climates gives them a little head start.

When harvesting make sure you snip off the fruit with scissors otherwise when you're trying to pull off the fruit, you might end up pulling out the whole plant (which happened to me with a cucumber once).

As I have said earlier, the pepper is truly a beautiful plant to grow and certainly has that "oooh-ahhh" factor for children and adults alike when the fruit starts off green (all varieties do), then turns into amazing colors of purple, red and orange.

PIQUILLO PEPPER, CHORIZO & MANGO SALAD WITH SEARED RARE TUNA

SERVES 4 AS AN ENTRÉE

This was a dish that was a highlight on the Circa menu when I first took over as head chef.
It is amazing how well fruit lends itself to savory dishes at times and this is one of them.
The mango really freshens up the rustic Mediterranean flavors of this dish.
Piquillo peppers can be purchased in most specialty food shops..

1 FRESH CHORIZO, PEELED AND CUT INTO ¾ INCH CUBES	2 TABLESPOONS FINELY CHOPPED ITALIAN PARSLEY
⅓ CUP GRAPESEED OIL	3 TABLESPOONS OLIVE OIL
½ MANGO, FINELY DICED	4 x 3 ½ OUNCES PIECES OF TUNA LOIN (ASK YOUR FISHMONGER TO PREP THESE FOR YOU WITHOUT ANY BLOODLINE)
½ SMALL RED ONION, FINELY DICED	
14 OUNCE JAR PIQUILLO PEPPERS, DRAINED AND FINELY DICED	SEA SALT AND FRESHLY GROUND BLACK PEPPER
JUICE OF 1 LEMON	1 CUP BABY WILD ARUGULA LEAVES

Heat a large skillet over medium heat. Once hot, add the chorizo and grapeseed oil and pan fry until colored on all sides, then take off the heat and strain, reserving the oil and chorizo. Set aside. The addition of the grapeseed oil will make a lovely dressing for the salad and garnish for the plate.

Place the mango, onion, peppers, half of the lemon juice and all the parsley in a large bowl and add enough of the reserved chorizo oil to bind everything. Arrange the salad onto each serving plate in a sporadic fashion. Arrange the cooked chorizo pieces around the plate as well.

Heat a large skillet over high heat. Add the olive oil and sear the tuna on one side until it is cooked halfway. Take off the heat, glaze the tuna with a little chorizo oil and the remaining lemon juice and season with salt and pepper. Place a piece of tuna onto each plate (or you could cut the tuna into 3 pieces first), then scatter over some arugula. Just before serving, drizzle the plate with a little more chorizo oil.

SIMPLE ROASTED PEPPERS
TURNED INTO ROMESCO SAUCE

MAKES ABOUT 3 CUPS OF SAUCE

This recipe is a nice and easy way to roast peppers. For the romesco sauce, I add quince paste to give it a sweet and earthy flavor. The sauce goes great with all pork dishes and vegetables and is also lovely with crayfish, but is just as delicious as a simple dip.

ROASTED PEPPERS

5 RED PEPPERS (ABOUT 1 POUND 14 OUNCES)

⅓ CUP OLIVE OIL

2 SPRIGS OREGANO

2 SPRIGS THYME

SEA SALT AND FRESHLY GROUND BLACK PEPPER

Preheat the oven to 425°F. Place all the ingredients in a roasting tray and mix together. Roast for 40–50 minutes, shaking every 8 minutes or so until the peppers become soft and the skins are nicely browned. Take out of the oven, cover with foil and leave to rest for 10 minutes. This keeps the moisture within the peppers and makes them easier to peel. After 10 minutes, carefully peel and remove all the seeds. Add the roasted flesh to salads or I like to turn it into romesco.

ROMESCO

1 POUND 5 OUNCES ROASTED PEPPER FLESH (NO SKIN OR SEEDS) (SEE RECIPE ABOVE)

⅓ CUP QUINCE PASTE

⅓ CUP ORGANIC RAW ALMONDS, BLANCHED IN BOILING WATER, THEN PEELED AND CHOPPED

1 GARLIC CLOVE

1 PINCH OF FENNEL SEEDS

1 PINCH OF CORIANDER SEEDS

1 PINCH OF NIGELLA SEEDS (ALSO KNOWN AS BLACK CUMIN OR KALONJI SEEDS)

1 PINCH OF CUMIN SEEDS

1 PINCH OF SUMAC

1 PINCH FINE SEA SALT

¾ CUP EXTRA VIRGIN OLIVE OIL

1 ½ TABLESPOONS CABERNET VINEGAR

Blitz the pepper flesh, quince paste, almonds and garlic to a purée in a food processor. Add the spices and salt and blitz again. Pour into a bowl, then fold in the oil and vinegar. It may require a little more vinegar to taste and some extra seasoning. This will keep well in the fridge for up to 1 week in an airtight container.

BAKED LONG GREEN PEPPERS, COUSCOUS & CURRANTS

SERVES 4

*One of my closest and best friends chef Nicolas Poelaert had a version of this dish
on his menu at Embrasse restaurant and I loved it that much I thought
I would interpret it into my own version, so here it is.*

½ CUP COUSCOUS

6 LONG GREEN SWEET PEPPERS
(ABOUT 9 OUNCES EACH)

1 TABLESPOON PUMPKIN SEEDS

1½ TABLESPOONS PINE NUTS

1½ TABLESPOONS CHOPPED ALMONDS

2 TABLESPOONS CURRANTS

1 TABLESPOON MINT LEAVES, CHOPPED

1 TABLESPOON ITALIAN PARSLEY
LEAVES, CHOPPED

2 TABLESPOONS EXTRA VIRGIN OLIVE OIL,
PLUS EXTRA FOR DRIZZLING

SEA SALT AND FRESHLY GROUND BLACK PEPPER

2¼ OUNCES HALOUMI, CUT INTO SMALL DICE

Preheat the oven to 375°F.

Place the couscous in a heatproof bowl and add ½ cup of water. Stir with a fork for 20 seconds, cover with plastic wrap and leave for 2–3 minutes, then stir again to release all the grains. Put to the side.

Trim the tops off the peppers, only ½–¾ inch from the top and set the tops aside. Insert a small knife inside the pepper and cut out the seeds and membrane. Turn upside down and shake or gently tap until all the seeds have fallen out.

Add the remaining ingredients to the couscous and mix thoroughly. Carefully spoon the mixture into the peppers, compacting it with your finger, then place the tops back on. Place in a small ovenproof baking dish and bake for 30–35 minutes or until the peppers are soft and browned. Take out of the tray and present on a platter to serve. I would highly recommend some simple salad leaves with this dish and, if you're feeling a wee adventurous, try with the tomato kasundi (see page 263).

CAROTENE

HARVEST
IN 12-18 WEEKS

Wild ancestors
from Afghanistan

first carrots were purple

grows well in deep
cool soil

VITAMIN (A)

CARROT

CARROT

Let me say this straight out—I love carrots. They are easily my favorite veg of all time.
Take the worst carrots you can possibly imagine—watery, overcooked, terrible mushy carrots
that you are fed in hospital—and I still just love them. In fact, I love them so much
I plan on getting a tattoo of one on my arm. Truly.

UNSUNG KITCHEN HEROES

There is so much more to this humble root than you might think. They are the unsung heroes of the kitchen. They're so versatile because of their natural sugar content, which means they cross the sweet/savory boundary effortlessly. They are an essential flavor base for broths and sauces and can be used in everything from stews and soups to cakes and preserves. They can be eaten raw, pickled, steamed, boiled, roasted, broiled, mashed, or even baked in salt. No wonder humans have been consuming carrots for thousands of years.

Before they were domesticated, the wild carrot was a tough, bitter root and only used medicinally. Wild carrot can still be found today and, though they are similar in taste and smell to domestic carrots, they are not related. I recommend that you don't go foraging for the wild kind as they closely resemble hemlock, which is poisonous, and the leaves can cause skin irritation. Best just to leave them alone.

Evidence exists, in the form of ancient cookbooks, that shows carrots were used in Roman cuisine, and it was through the expanding Roman Empire that they found their way onto the plates of Brits and the rest of Europe.

When you think of carrots, your mind immediately pictures vibrant orange. But originally orange wasn't the dominant color, it was a rarity. Where they were first domesticated, in Afghanistan, about 900 AD, carrots were sometimes white or yellow, but the most common color was purple.

The quintessential orange variety we now see in every supermarket wasn't widely cultivated until the 1500s in Northern Europe. Legend has it that gardeners from the Netherlands cultivated this color to honor William of Orange. This is a nice story though it's probably a myth, the color due instead to a naturally occurring mutation.

Steadily, this variety became more widely farmed, pushing out the other varieties to the fringes to become what we would now consider to be "heirloom" varieties.

Now, I know that a lot has been said and written regarding the "mass-produced versus small producer" or "chemical versus organic" vegetable argument, but I really believe the carrot is where you can honestly taste the difference, and it is worth the extra few dollars to buy organic. Try it yourself—buy one carrot from the supermarket and one from a farmers' market. Cut them in half; keep one half raw and cook the other half in salted boiling water until tender. Now shut your eyes and do a blind taste test of them—both raw and cooked. The difference is astonishing! The flavor that comes from the organic veg is delicate yet robust, so complex and sweet, and you'll be able to pick it over the dull mass-produced variety easily.

And that was what inspired my heirloom carrot salad, yogurt, almond and honey dressing (see page 84). It was the first dish that I considered to be my signature at Circa. It really represented my food philosophy.

GROWING

Here are some tips if you want to have a crack at growing carrots yourself. They are a great crop if you don't have a huge yard as they don't require a lot of space to produce a good yield. They love a sandy soil, but it has to be clean. Any little pebble or twig will split the carrot—they will just keep pushing down and end up growing around whatever is in their way.

Radishes are the ideal growing companions for carrots as they come up through the soil very rapidly and will break the surface to allow the more fragile carrot shoots to emerge unscathed.

If you accidentally pull up a carrot you've grown and find that it's a little immature, you can use the stalk. Just wash it and use it like you would parsley. It has a really interesting flavor and lovely foliage. Be adventurous and get your hands on some different shapes, sizes and colors—there are so many to choose from.

And here's one last little tip—you don't always need to peel carrots. If they are young and delicate, it's actually better not to. Just under the skin is where the majority of flavor is, so just

give them a wash or scrape with a scourer or the back of a knife and enjoy.

I've always grown them. I always will grow them, and you should too.

CARROT CAKE

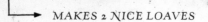

MAKES 2 NICE LOAVES

Now I have to thank my Brydie (she's like my little sister and has worked with me for five years) for this recipe. I have to, it's her little pot of gold. It's a winner and is on the Pope Joan cake display every day. It's always covered in sweetened cream cheese that has lemon juice added, and comes topped with chopped walnuts and pumpkin seeds. I wasn't really a fan of carrot cake before trying Brydie's recipe, but now I'm converted, especially when it's served with a wedge of brie and my fresh carrot pickle.

4 FREE-RANGE OR ORGANIC EGGS

1 ¾ CUPS SUPERFINE SUGAR

1 ¼ CUPS SUNFLOWER OIL

2 ¼ CUPS ALL-PURPOSE FLOUR

½ TEASPOON BAKING SODA

½ TEASPOON BAKING POWDER

1 PINCH OF GROUND CINNAMON

3 MEDIUM CARROTS, PEELED AND GRATED

2 CUPS WALNUTS, ROUGHLY CHOPPED

A WEDGE OF BRIE, AT ROOM TEMPERATURE, TO SERVE

GRATED CARROT, PRESERVED LEMON, RAISIN AND GINGER PICKLE (SEE PAGE 83), TO SERVE

Preheat the oven to 350°F. Grease two loaf tins (measuring 7 ½ x 3 ½ x 2 ½ inches) and line with parchment paper.

Whisk the eggs and sugar together until light and fluffy. Add the oil and mix in.

Strain the flour, baking soda, baking powder and cinnamon together. Mix into the egg mixture, then fold in the carrot and walnuts.

Pour into the loaf tins and bake for 30–45 minutes. To check if they're ready, use a skewer; it should ease through the mixture and come out without any cake batter on it. When cooked, turn out of the tins and place on a wire rack.

Cool to room temperature and serve with the brie and pickle. The cake is best eaten straight away. You can wrap it in plastic wrap and keep it in an airtight container for up to 4 days, but I recommend freezing what you can't eat and gently warming the defrosted cake in the oven.

GRATED CARROT, PRESERVED LEMON, RAISIN & GINGER PICKLE

FILLS AN 8-CUP CAPACITY JAR

This pickle is great with cold and hot meats, and also amazing with carrot cake and a wedge of brie (see page 80). In fact, it's great with all cheeses. I recommend making half the quantity if just serving with some brie.

1 CUP APPLE CIDER VINEGAR

1 ⅔ CUPS RICE WINE VINEGAR

⅔ CUP WHITE WINE

3 LARGE CARROTS, PEELED AND GRATED

2 ⅔ OUNCES PEELED AND GRATED GINGER (SO START WITH SAY 7 OUNCES)

1 CUP RAISINS

1 OUNCE PRESERVED LEMON (PEEL ONLY), THINLY SLICED

4 LARGE SHALLOTS, SLICED

¼ TEASPOON GROUND CORIANDER

1 TABLESPOON SEA SALT

Place all the liquids in a saucepan and bring to a boil, then add the rest of the ingredients. Remove from the heat, cover with parchment paper and allow to infuse until cool. Once cool, transfer to a sterilized 8-cup capacity jar with a lid.

This pickle is best served fresh on the day of making or the next, but it will keep well in the fridge for up to 3 months. As the pickle matures, the flavors will mellow.

HEIRLOOM CARROT SALAD, YOGURT, ALMOND & HONEY DRESSING

SERVES 4 AS AN ENTRÉE
OR AS A SALAD TO SHARE

Quite simply a beautiful dish. The almond and honey dressing really lifts the carrots to a new level. Please try it. This looks spectacular plated individually or on a big platter for the center of the table.

20 SMALL HEIRLOOM CARROTS (PURPLE, WHITE AND ORANGE VARIETIES OR JUST USE SMALL DUTCH CARROTS), WASHED AND TRIMMED (BUT NOT PEELED)

¾ CUP ORGANIC PLAIN YOGURT

½ BUNCH FENUGREEK OR PURSLANE, PICKED AND WASHED

8 SMALL NASTURTIUM LEAVES

8 NASTURTIUM FLOWERS (ANY COLOR)

ALMOND & HONEY DRESSING

¾ CUP ORGANIC RAW ALMONDS, ROUGHLY CHOPPED

3 TABLESPOONS BUTTER

3 TABLESPOONS HONEY (I USE ORANGE BLOSSOM)

1 TABLESPOON CHARDONNAY VINEGAR

1 TABLESPOON ORANGE-FLOWER WATER

JUICE OF 1 LEMON

1 LONG RED CHILI, SLICED

⅓ CUP EXTRA VIRGIN OLIVE OIL

SEA SALT

For the almond and honey dressing, place the almonds and butter in a 4-cup capacity saucepan. Place over medium heat and gently warm until the butter starts to foam. Keep it on the heat and when the butter turns a hazelnut color (beurre noisette), add the honey. Bring to a boil, then reduce by one-fifth. Add the vinegar, orange-flower water and lemon juice, bring back to the boil, turn down the heat and cook gently for 3 minutes. Pull off the heat, add the chili, olive oil and a pinch of salt and mix thoroughly. Set aside to cool. This dressing will keep in the fridge for up to 2 months—just gently warm before using.

Place the carrots in a saucepan of cold salted water and bring to a boil. Turn down to a simmer and cook for 8 minutes or until tender. Test the carrots with a sharp knife to see if they're cooked. Drain, then while the carrots are still hot, cut the larger ones in half, place in a bowl and toss in 3 tablespoons of the dressing.

To assemble, place one-quarter of the yogurt on each plate, then assemble the carrots on top. Dress with a little more dressing (making sure to scoop some of the almonds up) and scatter over the herbs and flowers.

Note If purslane, fenugreek and/or nasturtium leaves and flowers aren't readily available, you could just use Italian parsley, baby basil shoots and some small arugula leaves.

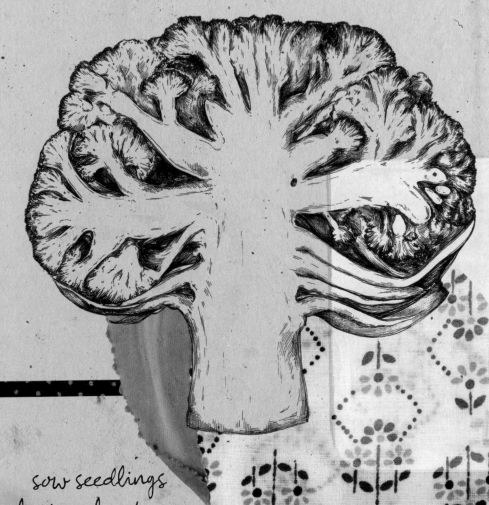

Has white, purple, green & orange varieties

sow seedlings with 16 inches between each plant

ALL YEAR ROUND Early Pearl EARLY SNOWBALL
VIOLETTA ITALIA WALCHEREN WINTER IGLOO

SOIL pH
IS IDEALLY "SWEET"
- NON ACIDIC

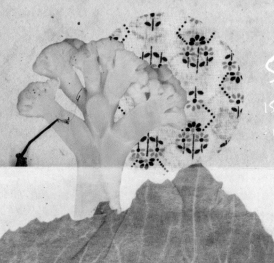

CAULIFLOWER

Cauliflower can be an annoying thing in
the garden because it takes up a lot of room.
But what would England be without cauliflower?

CAULIFLOWER

*I don't know too much about different cauliflower varieties, but I do know that I love it.
And I also know that, similar to globe artichokes and broccoli, the tighter the head the better it is.*

A MATTER OF NATIONAL PRIDE

Cauliflower is an annoying thing in the garden because it takes up a lot of room, like its ancestor, the cabbage. But I don't know what England would be without cauliflower—it is a national vegetable. We just love it. So many things that are made from it come to mind. National dishes like piccalilli, for example. Now I don't know one household in the whole of the UK that wouldn't have a jar of piccalilli in the fridge.

Cauliflower began its life as a subsidiary of the wild cabbage that was found growing uncultivated all around the ancient area of Asia Minor and from there it was traded as far as Turkey and Italy. By the sixteenth century it had found its way to France, where it became highly fashionable in the court of Louis XIV, and from there onto England.

VARIETIES

There are about 100 different varieties of cauliflower, but the two I am most familiar with are the All Year Round, which is cream colored with large florets, and Snowball, which has much smaller, more tightly packed florets and is also

much whiter. Then there are the baby caulis, which are so cute. They're a proper cauli, only miniature, being about the size of a tennis ball. They're great to use as a side to a roast or baked and served as individual cauliflower cheese. There are other colors of cauliflower available around the world, including orange, green and purple, which is quite common in Italy but harder to come by in the southern hemisphere—if it is overcooked the purple color will fade to green.

GROWING

My Grandad Tom used to grow two crops of cauli per year—one planted at the end of summer to be ready for winter and the second crop planted in winter for harvest in late spring. He'd wrap the leaves tightly around the flower head and even used to place a wet sack over them to help bleach them and make them whiter but also to keep dirt off the head. Cauliflower is also a member of the *Brassica genus*, as are broccoli and cabbage, which means that it will be fairly slow growing. The plants also take up a lot of room in your garden bed, so you will need to take a little time to think of where to place them and what you can plant in and around them to really make the most of the space in your beds.

You can put all your *Brassicas* in a bed together if you like, seeing they are all such large plants, but be warned: they can cross-pollinate with one another. To avoid this you will need to leave a bit of distance between varieties. In the past I have grown rows of parsnips or parsley in between.

COOKING

As I've mentioned with other *Brassica* family members (cabbage and Brussels sprouts in particular), poor old cauliflower has been on the receiving end of years of culinary abuse. I bet if you took a survey, one in ten people, be they kids or adults, would turn up their nose at lovely cauli and say, "Ugh, no, it stinks! It has a farty smell just like Brussels sprouts." I blame the bad cooking techniques of the past. If a kid is forced to eat limp overcooked veggies, how are they supposed to embrace them and enjoy them? They look, taste and smell disgusting. If kids have only ever had certain vegetables cooked poorly, how are they supposed to know how delightful they truly are? I guess that's how cauliflower cheese came to be—we had to try and disguise the taste and smell of all these limp overcooked veg.

Think about it. It still needs to be a little *al dente*, like its cousin broccoli. Not raw, but still retaining the integrity of the florets. Just as you would with pasta, cook cauliflower in salted boiling water until tender. Drain thoroughly, then let it sit for a minute or so in the colander and steam itself quite dry. You don't want to retain any of that cooking water on it because that is where the smell is. Add a knob of butter and some salt and pepper. Ooh, delicious. And that's it. It is so easy to make a beautiful vegetable like cauliflower appealing. Just cook it well and treat it with some respect.

Another way to enjoy cauli, which you may not have ever tried before, is raw. It is my favorite vegetable to eat raw. There is also a recipe for cauliflower with smoked salmon, strawberry and basil (see page 96). Strawberry and cauliflower may appear to be strange bedfellows, but trust me, it is so tasty. And again it's a raw style, which adds a lovely textural element to the dish. I do enjoy cauliflower every way—baked, boiled and pickled too—but raw cauli is just yum. One tip to keep in mind when enjoying it raw is to ensure you are cutting it very fine so it has a nice grit to it.

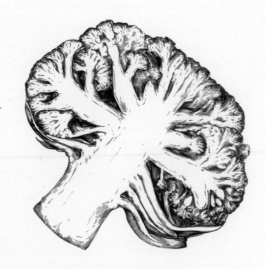

RAW, PICKLED & ROASTED CAULIFLOWER, WITH OR WITHOUT CRISPY SNAILS

SERVES 4 AS AN ENTRÉE

This salad certainly can be served without the snails for a lovely vegetarian option and you don't have to pickle and bake the cauliflower but all three textures and flavors of the cauliflower truly give this salad a little edge. If you are feeling brave, add some anchovies too.

CRISPY SNAILS

12-24 RAW SNAILS OUT OF THE SHELL (DEPENDING ON THE SIZE) (OPTIONAL)

1 BULB OF GARLIC, HALVED WIDTHWAYS

5 BLACK PEPPERCORNS

1 TABLESPOON FINE SEA SALT

2 SPRIGS ROSEMARY

PEEL AND JUICE OF 1 LEMON (PEEL REMOVED IN STRIPS AND WHITE PITH REMOVED)

3 TABLESPOONS OLIVE OIL

3 ½ TABLESPOONS BUTTER, DICED

1 GARLIC CLOVE, EXTRA, THINLY SLICED

1 TABLESPOON SALTED BABY CAPERS, RINSED

2 TABLESPOONS ITALIAN PARSLEY LEAVES, FINELY CHOPPED

CAULIFLOWER

1 LARGE HEAD CAULIFLOWER

3 TABLESPOONS OLIVE OIL

¾ CUP WHITE VINEGAR

1 TABLESPOON WHITE SUGAR

TO SERVE

5 AMARETTI BISCUITS (1 ½ OUNCES), ROUGHLY CHOPPED

2 CILANTRO STALKS, ROOTS ONLY, WASHED AND FINELY CHOPPED

5 SORREL LEAVES, SHREDDED

1 LARGE SHALLOT, FINELY CHOPPED

½ POMEGRANATE, SEEDS REMOVED (USE ONLY IF IN SEASON)

4 TABLESPOONS HOUSE VINAIGRETTE (SEE PAGE 279)

SEA SALT AND FRESHLY GROUND BLACK PEPPER

4 TABLESPOONS SOFT, FRESH GOAT CHEESE OR FROMAGE BLANC

For the crispy snails, place the snails, garlic bulb halves, peppercorns, salt, rosemary and lemon peel into an 8-cup capacity saucepan and add enough water to cover the ingredients by 2 inches. Bring to a boil, then reduce to a simmer and cook for 40 minutes. Remove from the heat and leave in the liquid until cooled, then remove the snails with a slotted spoon and pat dry on paper towels. Discard the poaching liquid and solids.

For the cauliflower, preheat the oven to 400°F. Remove the florets from the head of cauliflower and reserve the stalk. Chop half of the cauliflower florets into pinky-fingernail-sized pieces and place in a roasting tray with the olive oil and roast for 15–20 minutes, shaking the tray occasionally until the cauliflower is light golden. Take out of the oven and place in a large bowl.

Place the vinegar, sugar and ½ cup of water in a saucepan, bring to a boil, then take off the heat. Finely chop the reserved stalk and chop half of the remaining cauliflower florets into baby pea-sized pieces and add both to the pickling liquid. Set aside until ready to serve.

Finely chop the remaining cauliflower florets and add to the roasted cauliflower.

To serve, add the amaretti biscuit, cilantro root, sorrel, shallot and half of the pomegranate seeds to the bowl of cauliflower and mix in.

Drain the pickled cauliflower and add to the bowl along with the house vinaigrette. Season with salt and pepper and toss to combine. Arrange on plates, spoon over the goat cheese and scatter over the remaining pomegranate seeds.

To finish the crispy snails, heat a large skillet over high heat, add the olive oil and snails and pan fry for 4–6 minutes or until crispy. Add the butter and turn down the heat to low. Add the sliced garlic, capers and parsley and continue cooking until the butter has turned to a light brown color. Add the lemon juice, then take off the heat. Place the snails over the cauliflower salad and spoon over a little of the cooking juices.

PICCALILLI

FILLS 8 STANDARD PRESERVING JARS

'Piccalilli, it's luminous. Never eat anything luminous.' English comedian Peter Kay's description of this classic English pickle always makes me cry with laughter. I have many fond memories as a young'un eating ham and piccalilli sandwiches.

9 OUNCES COOKING SALT

1 LARGE HEAD CAULIFLOWER FLORETS

4 LARGE ZUCCHINI,
CHOPPED INTO PIECES THE SIZE OF
THE END OF YOUR THUMB

2 LARGE TURNIPS, CHOPPED INTO
THUMB-SIZED PIECES

3 WHITE ONIONS,
HALVED AND SLICED

½ CUP ALL-PURPOSE FLOUR

1 ¾ TABLESPOONS GROUND TURMERIC

1 CUP WHITE SUGAR

5 CUPS APPLE CIDER VINEGAR

Bring 8 ½ cups of water and the salt to the boil in a 16-cup capacity saucepan, then allow to cool. Once cool, add all the vegetables and leave to pickle for 12 hours or overnight.

The next day, bring to a boil and boil gently for 15 minutes. Drain, then add the vegetables back to the pot.

Place the flour, turmeric and sugar in a large mixing bowl and whisk in 1 cup of the vinegar to make a paste. Whisk until there are no lumps, then add the remaining vinegar. Add to the vegetables and cook over high heat for 15 minutes, stirring every minute or so. Take off the heat and let stand until cooled to room temperature.

Meanwhile, sterilize eight standard preserving jars with lids. Transfer the piccalilli mix into the jars and store in your cupboard for at least 3 weeks or longer before using. Unopened jars will keep for a good year or two. Store opened jars in the fridge for up to 3 months.

SALAD OF CAULIFLOWER, SMOKED SALMON & STRAWBERRY

SERVES 4

It is important to get the balance right in this dish. The freshly cracked pepper brings out the flavor of the strawberries so you really need to taste it—add pepper as if you were an old man peppering his soup. It may seem like an odd pairing but the strawberry flavor blends subtly with the smoked salmon and cauliflower. The lemon juice adds acid, the cauliflower adds an earthy flavor while the sour cream gives a lovely mouthfeel. This is delicious on its own, great as a side for simple baked fish, or as a shared entrée. But it's also brilliant as a canapé to get the tastebuds gurgling with a nice glass of Champagne. How could you resist? Please give me a glass now.

2 SMALL HEADS CAULIFLOWER

3 ½ OUNCES SMOKED SALMON, DICED

5 LARGE STRAWBERRIES, SHUCKED AND DICED

3 SHALLOTS, FINELY DICED

3 SORREL LEAVES, FINELY SHREDDED

SEA SALT AND FRESHLY GROUND BLACK PEPPER

JUICE OF 2 SMALL LEMONS

3 TABLESPOONS HAZELNUT OIL
(OR SUBSTITUTE EXTRA VIRGIN OLIVE OIL)

⅔ CUP SOUR CREAM

1 BUNCH BASIL SHOOTS, TRIMMED,
OR 10 BASIL LEAVES, THINLY SLICED

With a sharp knife, carefully remove the florets from the cauliflower and shred them. Discard the stalk (or, because we hate waste, make a soup out of it). Place the florets in a large bowl and gently combine with the smoked salmon, strawberries, shallot and sorrel. Season with salt and a good grind of pepper to bring out the strawberries.

Just before serving, add the lemon juice and oil. Place in a serving dish, place 1 teaspoonful dollops of the sour cream around the top and scatter over the basil shoots.

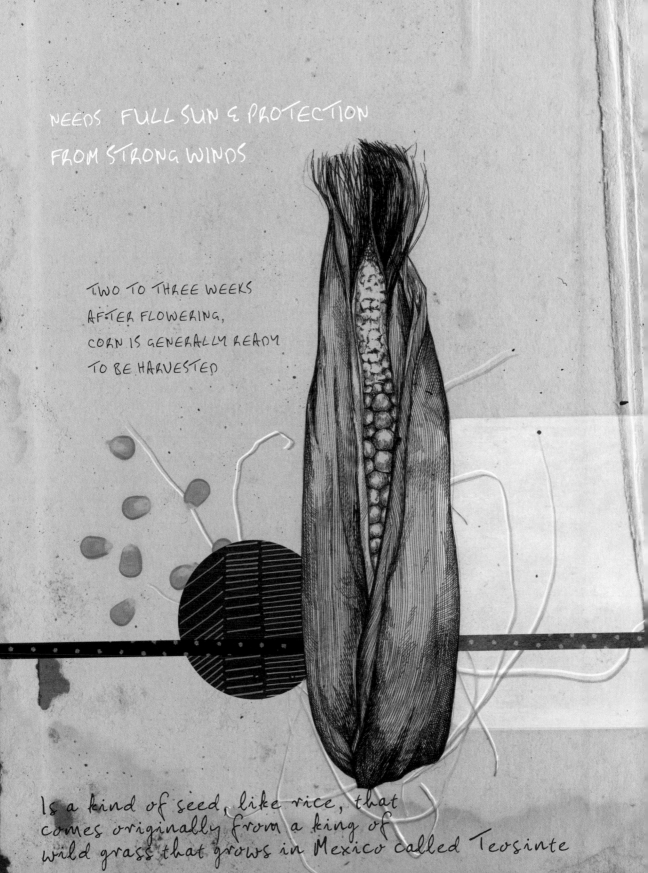

NEEDS FULL SUN & PROTECTION
FROM STRONG WINDS

TWO TO THREE WEEKS
AFTER FLOWERING,
CORN IS GENERALLY READY
TO BE HARVESTED

Is a kind of seed, like rice, that
comes originally from a king of
wild grass that grows in Mexico called Teosinte

Corn is so firmly embedded in world cuisine that it's hard to remember that it's only been on European and Asian tables since the 1500s. Could you imagine a Chinese menu without chicken and corn soup?

CORN

The Iroquis gave the first recorded corn (called Papoon) to European settlers in 1779.

CORN

*Unlike a lot of other vegetables, which I came to love and appreciate in later life,
I've always had a soft spot for corn. To me it will always bring back images of the local fair
or carnival when I was a kid, annoying Dad to give me some money so I could go to the stall
and get corn on the cob, impaled on a stick, steaming and dripping with butter.
There's nothing quite like it! And it was much better value for money than all the sideshows.*

THE FRESHER THE SWEETER

Even after I came to Australia as an adult,
I would always get a corn on the cob to eat as
I was walking around the Queen Victoria Market
in Melbourne. I tend to think of it as a "meaty"
vegetable—I mean, there is no delicate way to
eat corn on the cob. As with lamb chops, you
have to get in there and use your hands, really get
involved. That's what makes it so fun.

There is an old saying that corn picked longer
than two hours has lost all its flavor. This could
be true, as I have many a time picked the knobbly
bugger, cooked her straight away and the flavor
is truly intense. Fresh just-picked corn has that
slight natural licorice flavor to it that seems to
disappear after a few hours, but if you know a
corn grower, like I do, ask him to pick the baby
immature corn for you and leave the husk on it—
these should keep longer and retain a little of the
licorice flavor.

When explorer Christopher Columbus
discovered the Americas he also "discovered"
corn, which is also known by the aliases maize and

corn, depending on where you are in the world.
Corn, which is actually considered a grass, not a
grain, was a staple of the indigenous peoples of
South America, although it looked a lot different
to the tightly packed cobs that we know today and
more like a kind of wheat. The Europeans would
probably not have survived on the inhospitable
American shores if they hadn't embraced this
versatile vegetable and learned from the natives
how to cultivate and tend their crop.

NOT JUST FOR EATING

Now corn is so firmly embedded in world cuisine
that it's hard to remember that it's only been on
European and Asian tables since the 1500s.
Could you imagine a Chinese menu without
chicken and corn soup? Or Italy without polenta?
It has been embraced right across the world
from Mexico to Africa, especially among the
poorer nations as a valuable source of protein,
carbohydrates and vitamins.

But here is something to think about—you have
probably never realized that not a day goes by
without you eating corn or a derivative of it in

some shape or form, which is not so surprizing as corn is at the top of the world's seven most farmed crops. But what form the corn takes is the surprizing part. I mean, I love Mars bars, but only recently realized they were made from corn, with corn syrup being one of the main sweeteners. There are more than 3,000 products that are made from or contain corn, including the more obvious food items like cornmeal (also known as polenta), cornstarch, popcorn, cornbread, corn chips, tortillas, Southern American specialty foods likes grits and hominy, and Dr Kellogg's most famous invention, Corn Flakes. But there are a lot of products that have less obvious uses for corn, and most of them aren't culinary. There are baby powders, fuels, plastics, paper, batteries, cosmetics, insecticides, toothpastes, textiles and explosives. And that's just a few from a seriously long list. It is so much more than the readily available veg.

GROWING

For now, though, let's forget about mass-production and think about a small plot and how to get the best results. I first tried to grow corn about seven years ago. It wasn't a roaring success. What little ears I did manage to grow were small and patchy, with not many kernels at all. I think I was too concerned with spacing and didn't really think about the fact that corn isn't a self-pollinating plant. It needs our help for the male part, which is the top-most flowering section, to pollinate the female, which is the part that becomes the fruit. So with the next plot I tried, I really just crowded the seeds together and I didn't thin the plants out because I knew now that as they mature the motion of them brushing against one another is what is going to give you more fruit.

Experiment with different types and colors of corn. Move away from plain old yellow and get into white, red and black corn or even a mixture. There are so many different heirloom varieties to choose from. The best thing is that after a successful crop, all you need to do is save a couple of ears and dry out the kernels in a warm spot, or low oven, and you will have seeds for the following year. You'll find there's nothing quite like the sweetness of those milky kernels plucked straight from the plant and eaten fresh. Amazing.

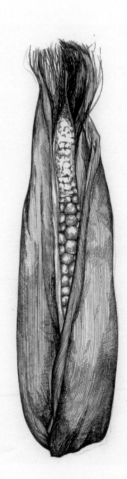

FRESH BABY CORN, HERB SALT & BUTTER

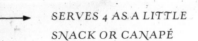

Baby corn is essential for this and it needs to be fresh and in season.
Make sure you buy ears with the husks still on so the corn stays sweeter and fresher.
It's important to serve the corn warm to get that small hint
of licorice flavor from them.

16 EARS BABY CORN, HUSKS REMOVED	**HERB SALT (SEE PAGE 279), FOR SPRINKLING**
3 TABLESPOONS BUTTER, MELTED	

Cook the corn in salted boiling water over medium heat for 5–7 minutes. You want the corn to still be a little crisp. Drain and place the corn in a bowl, add the butter and herb salt and toss to coat.

FRESH CORN SALAD, SHRIMP, JALAPEÑO, RED ONION & CRÈME FRAÎCHE

SERVES 4 AS A MAIN

This is a dish I have made in various forms many a time but I tried and tested this version on two good friends, Jenni Draper and Rosanne Hyland, my former bosses from Circa, so the pressure was on. Luckily all went well and they heartily agreed with me that this is a truly splendid main-course salad, so fresh and flavorsome.

2 EARS CORN, HUSKS REMOVED

SEA SALT AND FRESHLY GROUND BLACK PEPPER

1 ⅔ CUPS SUNFLOWER OIL

1 SPRIG TARRAGON

12 RAW LARGE SHRIMP, PEELED AND DEVEINED

2 TABLESPOONS PICKLED JALAPEÑO, ROUGHLY CHOPPED

¼ RED ONION, THINLY SLICED

1 SHORT CUCUMBER, QUARTERED AND CUT INTO CHUNKS

2 TABLESPOONS CRÈME FRAÎCHE

JUICE OF ½ LEMON

3 SCALLIONS, THINLY SLICED

2 TABLESPOONS MINT LEAVES, SHREDDED

1 BUNCH SMALL-LEAF CILANTRO

Fill a saucepan with 6 cups of water, add the corn and some salt and bring to a boil, then reduce to a simmer and cook for 9–12 minutes. Once cooked, take off the heat and allow the corn to cool in the liquid, then shave the kernels from the cobs, using a sharp knife, and place into a large bowl. Discard the cooking water and ears or save to make a broth (see Note).

Place the sunflower oil and tarragon in a 4-cup capacity saucepan and bring to a simmer, then immediately take off the heat and add the shrimp. Leave for 5–10 minutes. You only want to slightly confit the shrimp. You can, if you like, steam the shrimp. Remove with a slotted spoon.

Add the jalapeño, onion, cucumber, crème fraîche and 8 of the shrimp along with 1 teaspoon of the confit oil, lemon juice, season with salt and pepper and mix gently. Mix in half of the scallion, mint and cilantro. Arrange on a plate and top with the rest of the shrimp, scallion and herbs.

Note Add the cobs of the corn back to the saucepan of cooking water and simmer for 6–10 minutes or until the flavor has intensified. Now, you have a beautiful vegetarian broth to use in soups or purées.

NONNA LEAH'S CORNBREAD

MAKES ABOUT 30 TRIANGLES

A fantastic afternoon snack out in the backyard overlooking the garden,
or simply substitute for toast with your breakfast.

CREAMED CORN

- 3 EARS FRESHLY SHAVED CORN KERNELS
- 1 GENEROUS CUP LIGHT CREAM

CORNBREAD

- ½ CUP BUTTER
- 1 RED ONION, FINELY DICED
- 1 TABLESPOON SWEET CHILI SAUCE
- 1 FREE-RANGE OR ORGANIC EGG

- ¾ CUP MILK
- 3 TABLESPOONS BUTTERMILK
- 12 OUNCES CREAMED CORN (SEE ABOVE)
- 1 CUP POLENTA
- 1 CUP ALL-PURPOSE FLOUR, SIFTED
- 1 ½ TEASPOONS BAKING POWDER
- ½ TEASPOON COOKING SALT
- ⅔ CUP CHEDDAR, GRATED

For the creamed corn, place the corn and cream in a 4-cup capacity saucepan and bring to a boil. Turn down the heat to a simmer and cook for 40–50 minutes. Cool slightly, then transfer to a food processor and blitz until smooth. Transfer into a container and chill until ready to serve. This is also great just as a corn purée. (Makes 12 ounces.)

For the cornbread, preheat the oven to 350°F and lightly grease a baking dish (measuring 12 x 7 ½ x 2 ½ inches).

Melt the butter in a skillet over medium heat. Add the onion and cook until softened. Add the sweet chili sauce and heat through.

Whisk the egg, milk and buttermilk together in a bowl, then stir in the creamed corn.

Mix the polenta, flour, baking powder and salt in a large bowl. Add the egg mixture, onion mixture and cheese. Pour into the baking dish and bake for 60–65 minutes. Test with a skewer to see if it's ready, then remove from the dish and leave to cool slightly on a wire rack. Portion into small triangles and serve straight away as a little snack in the afternoon. It will keep wrapped in parchment paper and stored in an airtight container for up to 1 week.

SOFT PARMESAN POLENTA
WITH CRAB & MUSSELS

SERVES 4

This is one of those dishes that came about because of a mistake I made while cooking at home. I had used far too much liquid to cook my polenta but it turned into a beauty of a dish. I added mascarpone and Parmesan, some shrimp and mussels and voila! I served it with a simple arugula salad—it needs the fresh bite of some salad leaves to accompany it. The next day at Circa, I played around with the dish and a week later it was on the menu. It's now one of my favorite dishes to make and marries amazingly with a glass of chardonnay. I like to serve it in a copper pan in the middle of the table and let people help themselves, then freshly slice truffle over the top (that is when truffles are in season and I've had a lucky day at the races).

2 POUNDS 4 OUNCES LOCAL MUSSELS, DEBEARDED AND CLEANED

1 ⅔ CUPS WHITE WINE

10 ½ OUNCES COOKED CRABMEAT, PICKED OVER AND CHECKED FOR ANY SHELL

1 CUP INSTANT POLENTA

PINCH FINE SEA SALT

25 TURNS OF BLACK PEPPER FROM A MILL

½ CUP FINELY GRATED PARMESAN

2 TABLESPOONS TRUFFLE OIL

1 TABLESPOON MASCARPONE

2 TABLESPOONS CHERVIL LEAVES, CHOPPED

2 TABLESPOONS ITALIAN PARSLEY LEAVES, CHOPPED

JUICE OF 1 LEMON

Heat a 8-cup capacity saucepan over high heat and heat for 1 minute or so until hot, then add the mussels (you should be able to hear them bubbling) and stir for 2 minutes. Add the wine, put the lid on and cook for exactly 5 minutes. Take off the heat and pass through a fine strainer, reserving the mussel cooking liquid for later. While the mussels are warm, take the meat out of the shells, removing any stray pieces of beard or grit. Roughly chop the mussel meat and combine with the crabmeat.

Rinse out the pan you used to cook the mussels. Add the polenta and 2 cups of the reserved mussel cooking water and also 2 cups of water and cook, stirring all the time, over medium heat. Stir for about 6-9 minutes or until you cannot feel any grains on your tongue when you taste it. The consistency you're after is a smooth soft-cooked polenta kind of like porridge. Now, turn down the heat to low, add the salt, pepper and Parmesan and cook until the cheese has melted into the mixture. Take off the heat, stir in the mussel and crab mixture and the rest of the ingredients and serve straight away. I'd recommend a salad with this to cut the richness of it; try the shaved fennel and mozzarella salad with braised goat neck on page 140 or the simple pick your own salad on page 172.

MORE
THAN
WATER

NEED LOOSE, WELL DRAINED SOIL
WITH PLENTY OF ORGANIC MATTER

originally from INDIA where
they have been cultivated for
at least 3000 years.

CUCUMBER

are thirsty plants and are susceptible
to fungal infection

(CUCUMIS SATIVUS)

CUCUMBER

Cucumber is one of those things I hadn't seen growing in my youth apart from one time in an allotment. When I first saw a vine with beautiful yellow flowers I thought I was looking at a small cactus; it looked so spiny and sharp.

VARIETIES

There are many different kinds of cucumber, and more heritage (heirloom) breeds are emerging. Cucumbers can all pretty much be divided into four categories based on what use they are most suited to. The first is slicing, which are obviously the best to simply slice and serve raw in salads. They are suited to most cucumber recipes. Category two is pickling—fairly self-explanatory. This is the category where gherkins live. Burpless cucumber is category three, and, although it seems quite funny, obviously the non-social behavior invoked by your cucumber of old was enough to make some polite farmer or scientist take the time to produce varieties that won't repeat on you. Bless them. And, finally, there is specialty, which include all heritage varieties. But still, if you stopped someone in the street and asked them to name some cucumber varieties, they could probably only tell you two— small and continental—off the top of their head. These are the universal ones, the all-rounders, and you will find them in every supermarket. But it is really worth keeping an eye out for different kinds. Go to a farmers' market and there are so many different varietals out there. Try the Crystal Apple, developed by Arthur Yates in Sydney in

the thirties. It has an unusual oval shape, with creamy white flesh, and is really quite lovely. Or the Armenian, which is long, like a gourd, and sometimes called a "snake melon." Then there are the Jefferson and Syrian, which have yellow skin and are round like apples. Different varieties have lots of different characteristics and flavors. Some have bitter skin but soft creamy flesh, some have heaps of seeds and hardly any flesh at all, and some have an incredibly high water content. They all suit different uses. This is why I love growing my own, and why it is worth putting a little bit of time into researching different varieties. A website like *http://sustainableseedco.com* is great for this as not only do they stock many hard to find heirloom seeds, they also can give you some tips on how to get the best growing results.

USES

You wouldn't think it at first but the humble cuc is another world-conquering veggie. It originated in India, where it is hailed for its wonderful refreshing and cooling properties, and is made into the beautiful yogurt dip, raita, which is served as a foil alongside fiery curries. In India during colonial times it must have been a godsend to all those English gentlemen, and they then adopted it and took it home with them. I mean there's nothing more British than a cucumber sandwich, is there? But also, the Japanese love soured and pickled cucumber, the French adore their cornichons—the tiny refined pickled cucumbers—the Polish and Germans love their gherkins. And honestly what would a corned beef and sauerkraut roll be without sweet gherkins? Or a Big Mac, for that matter? It's quite funny to think that the great linguist Samuel Johnson held such a low opinion of them that he is credited to have said, "... a cucumber should be well sliced, and dressed with pepper and vinegar, and then thrown out, as good for nothing." How rude!

PREPARING

Now I am going to broach some subjects that have been the issue of debates for many a long year: to salt or not to salt? To peel or not to peel? Well, these are the questions. And my answers are, really, it's up to you. Except if you're making cucumber sandwiches, in which case you must peel. I don't think HM the Queen would be having a bar of afternoon tea if she found the cucumber in her sandwiches still had the skin on! No, really, I find that there are some cucumber varieties that have quite coarse and bitter skin, so I would recommend peeling, in that case. However, you want to peel very finely and not remove too much of the lovely green pigment that is just under the skin. Salting again is a matter of taste, but I think that everything can benefit from a little judicious seasoning. And, as I will discuss further with zucchini (see pages 264–75), salting the cucumber flesh can draw out any excess moisture, which can be beneficial.

GROWING

When you are looking to grow your own cucumbers, it's handy to know that they do like a nice amount of lime in the soil, and they don't need a lot of manure. They also perform best with a mid-level or neutral pH in the soil, which means not too acidic but not too alkaline either. And boy, do they love water! It makes sense, really, as they do have such a high water content.

Please try to grow them from seed—it's so satisfying to put seedlings in your little hothouse, and then transplant them to the garden. Make a teepee of garden stakes so that their vines have something to grip onto and climb up. You can put at least 5–6 seedlings around each teepee. One thing to be mindful of, and it's something I've done a few times and been quite angry at myself for, cucumbers have very small, fine root systems so when pulling the fruit be gentle. Otherwise you will pull the whole plant out, and then you'll be annoyed at yourself. And if you do accidentally do it, don't try to replant it. It doesn't work— trust me.

CUCUMBER & YOGURT SOUP

SERVES 4

You may not be a fan of cold soups (I know my missus isn't) but think of them as a sauce that marries beautifully with other things or a refreshing cleanser on a warm day. This is one of my favorite cold soups: velvety, creamy and delicious. It goes brilliantly with picked crabmeat, crayfish or poached chicken. Try adding some nuts to it or golden raisins and, if the flavor is lacking a little, add a dash of red wine vinegar or lemon juice to round out the flavors.

¾ CUP UNSALTED BUTTER

3 LARGE CONTINENTAL CUCUMBERS, PEELED, SEEDS REMOVED AND ROUGHLY CHOPPED

1 ¼ CUPS SHEEP'S MILK YOGURT

SEA SALT AND FRESHLY GROUND BLACK PEPPER

EXTRA VIRGIN OLIVE OIL, TO SERVE

Melt the butter in a large heavy-bottomed saucepan over medium heat. Add the cucumber and gently sauté for 7–10 minutes, without any coloring, or until the cucumber starts to soften. Immediately pour the mixture into a blender and blitz until smooth. Pass through a fine strainer into a bowl and refrigerate until chilled.

Once chilled, gently whisk in the yogurt, season with salt and pepper and pass again through a fine strainer. Serve immediately, with a drizzle of extra virgin olive oil, or chill again until ready to use.

IRENE'S TZATZIKI

Irene is a lovely Greek lady who works for Thermomix Australia. She attended a cooking class of mine at Tony Tan's Unlimited Cuisine Company in Melbourne, and then she came to eat at Pope Joan. She ordered one of my salads and told me it was delicious but some tzatziki would have really lifted the dish. Me being a stubborn Yorkshire fellow, I turned up my nose. But Irene was not put off. She went on to tell me that it's not just about throwing all the ingredients together to make a tzatziki, they should be incorporated gradually to maximize the flavor.

I tried it and she was right. When done properly, it is far superior to the bought stuff and I now add it to all sorts of things. I recommend making this a day ahead to allow the flavors to develop. Thanks Irene, you're a champ.

2 CUPS THICK SHEEP'S MILK YOGURT

1 LARGE CONTINENTAL CUCUMBER, PEELED, GRATED AND THE EXCESS WATER SQUEEZED OUT

1 TABLESPOON ITALIAN PARSLEY LEAVES, CHOPPED

1 TABLESPOON DILL, FINELY CHOPPED

1 ½ TABLESPOONS WHITE VINEGAR

2 TABLESPOONS OLIVE OIL

2 PINCHES OF FINE SEA SALT

15 TURNS OF WHITE PEPPER FROM A MILL

3 GARLIC CLOVES, FINELY GRATED ON A MICROPLANE

Place the yogurt, cucumber, parsley and dill in a bowl and gently fold together.

Next, you need to build the flavors gradually. Start by folding in the vinegar, oil, salt and pepper. Taste to see if a little more vinegar or salt is needed. Now slowly incorporate as much garlic as you like. The flavor of the garlic will intensify while it sits in the fridge so less is more.

ROASTED CUCUMBER, QUINOA, FREEKAH & HERBS

MAKES A NICE BIG SALAD FOR 4

Roasted cucumber? You must think I'm crazy! Well, this is a delightful salad, perfect for summer.

A must-try while sipping a gin and tonic..

3 SMALL CUCUMBERS, PEELED, SEEDS REMOVED, QUARTERED AND CUT INTO 1 ¼ INCH PIECES

1 TEASPOON FINE SEA SALT

3 TABLESPOONS OLIVE OIL

1 ½ CUPS COOKED QUINOA (MIXED OR JUST ONE TYPE) (SEE PAGE 276)

½ CUP COOKED FREEKAH (SEE PAGE 276)

¼ RED ONION, THINLY SLICED

3 TABLESPOONS ORGANIC RAW ALMONDS, CHOPPED

3 TABLESPOONS GOLDEN RAISINS

3 TABLESPOONS SUNFLOWER SEEDS

JUICE OF 1 LEMON

⅓ CUP EXTRA VIRGIN OLIVE OIL

1 TABLESPOON ITALIAN PARSLEY LEAVES, CHOPPED

1 TABLESPOON MINT LEAVES, CHOPPED

½ CUP PICKED WATERCRESS

SEA SALT AND FRESHLY GROUND BLACK PEPPER

¾ CUP NATURAL YOGURT

Place the cucumber on a tray lined with a paper towel and sprinkle liberally with the salt. Let stand for 3 minutes, then rinse and pat dry with some more paper towels. This is to draw out the moisture of the cucumber so as to not make your salad soggy.

Heat a large skillet over high heat, add the olive oil and cucumber and pan fry for about 4 minutes or until the cucumber is golden brown. Place in a bowl (I'd use the same bowl that you would like to present the salad in).

Add the remaining ingredients to the bowl, except the yogurt and reserve a little of the herbs. Gently toss together and check the seasoning. To finish, spoon the yogurt over the top in small dollops, then sprinkle with the reserved herbs.

X don't like
FROST

It is a delicate perennial
often cultivated as an annual

originated in India and cultivated
in China from as early as 600BC

DIDN'T BECOME POPULAR
IN AUSTRALIA UNTILL THE
ARRIVAL OF EUROPEAN
MIGRANTS IN THE 1950S

EGGPLANT

VERY RICH IN
VITAMIN B6

EGGPLANT

*I've been in Australia ten years now, but it still irks me calling aubergine eggplant—
I can't get used to it. In the UK, it is known as aubergine. And why is it called
eggplant anyway? It's purple, not white! Well, the name comes from
the now little-known white variety, which does very closely resemble an egg.*

SUMMER BELLA DONNA

Eggplant is a weird vegetable to me, right up there with zucchini and some of the other Mediterranean veggies that I really didn't like until I moved to Australia. I think eggplant was overused when I was growing up, and I didn't really like the flavor of it. I found it to be very sour and astringent on my palate, but that was really only because I'd overcooked and badly prepared it.

Trying a really good baba ghanoush is what changed my mind. It was amazing; so creamy and smoky, served on some warm crispy pita bread. Just delicious! Once you've tried that, how can you not love eggplant? If only Dad or Mum had given me baba ghanoush as a kid, maybe I would have enjoyed it more.

It was only nine years ago, when I began visiting Arnie and Jo Pizzini, owners of Chrismont winery in the King Valley in country Victoria, when I really began to understand and appreciate the Italian way of cooking eggplant. I was trained in the French tradition and I didn't really understand the simplicity of flavor in Italian cooking. Arnie and Jo's background is half-Sicilian

and half-Milanese, and it was eating Jo's mom's, Nonna Franca's, Sicilian-style eggplant (see page 125) that opened my eyes to everything eggplant could be when prepared with love and respect for the vegetable itself. It was simply salted, then broiled and marinated with vinegar, oil, garlic (of course) and seasoning, then finished with some chopped basil. We sat down to eat and around the dinner table there were also meatballs, salads, lasagne ... Of course in the style of true Italian hospitality, there was more food than you can imagine—but it was the eggplant I really fell in love with. I couldn't get enough. And now I eat a lot of it—through summer, that is. It is a beautiful summer veg and should be kept as a summer veg. I think it's very similar to tomato in that way, and I try my best to eat it only when it's at its peak.

VARIETIES

There are many different varietals out there. Three that I know of, just off the top of my head, are the Black Beauty, which is the large purple kind you will find in the supermarket. Then there is the Lebanese eggplant, which looks like a long purple finger. They are great to simply slice, lightly salt and pan fry. Rosa Bianca is a light pink/purple mottled one that is very beautiful to look at. There are also some Indian varieties, which are a multicolored mottle. And then there's white, as I mentioned before, which are called Japanese White Egg.

USES AND EATING

Eggplant is another far-reaching veg. It was originally cultivated in India and didn't receive great acclaim when it was first introduced into Britain as it suffered from guilt by association, being distantly related to the deadly nightshade. And for some unknown reason, it was thought to cause all manner of ailments, from a poor complexion to leprosy and piles. But part of its rise to popularity may be explained in the translation of its Sanskrit name, vatin-gana, which means "anti-wind" or "wind-killer." So it came to be used as a great foil to any diet that was high in wind-causing vegetables, such as beans or cabbage.

The Japanese just love it dressed with sweet miso, and it stars in many Indian curries. Imagine the Syrians and Lebanese without eggplant—just like Mork without Mindy. It is a mainstay of Italian cuisine, being one of the essential ratatouille vegetables, and Greeks, with their famous national dish, moussaka, would also be quite lost without it.

GROWING

It was around nine years ago that I grew my first eggplant. And, you know, I'm a little embarrassed to say, I felt quite like a child when you ask them where a potato comes from and they don't know it comes from the ground. When I first planted the seedling I was very excited but didn't really know what to expect. The plant got bigger and

bigger and was soon up to my knees, and then it stopped. Then a beautiful purple flower came out with a big bud, and after a few weeks the bud had become a huge eggplant, attached by this one scrawny looking stalk. I thought, "Imagine being an eggplant out there in the garden, everyone looking at you. Surely you'd be the 'chicken legs' of the garden world—kind of like my skinny legs. All the other plants would be laughing at you!" It is a beautiful fruit, but also quite a comical one with its massive bulbous growth coming from a spindly little stalk.

When you are planting, remember that eggplants need full sun, and they need to be spaced about 8 inches apart. I find the best results are if you grow to seedling in a little hotbox, which are readily available at good nurseries or hardware shops. Once they've reached about 2½ inches high they are ready to be transplanted into the garden. Put a lot of straw around the base of the plant as it is greedy with water and the straw will help keep it moist. Four to five seedlings will be enough for a good crop and they are a pretty plant. Kids will be amazed, and even you will be too, at just how the little chicken legs manage to hold up the equivalent of a medicine ball.

SICILIAN-STYLE SALTED & VINEGARED EGGPLANT IN A SANDWICH WITH MOZZARELLA & BASIL

MAKES 8 SMALL OR 4 LARGE

This recipe marries two great food memories of my life: eggplant and the best sandwiches. The first memory comes from when I visited my good friends Arnie and Jo Pizzini at Chrismont winery in the King Valley. They cook so beautifully and it wasn't until I tried this version of cooked eggplant that I came to enjoy the veg. The other memory comes from spending many great times as a child with my relatives, particularly Aunty Mary and Uncle Pete, in different coal-mining villages of Barnsley, where I ate the best sandwiches ever. What made them so special? It was all to do with the bread. Well, the filling and pickles that went with the sandwiches were great too, but the bread was in a league of its own—it was the classic Yorkshire teacake style: soft and fluffy and it left your lips covered in flour like a doughnut leaves sugar. You may want to elaborate on my sandwich, adding whatever ingredients go well together.

EGGPLANT

1 LARGE EGGPLANT, THINLY SLICED FROM TIP TO TOE

1 ½ TABLESPOONS FINE SEA SALT

1 ½ TABLESPOONS OLIVE OIL

2 GARLIC CLOVES, SLICED

1 ¼ CUPS EXCEPTIONAL WHITE WINE VINEGAR (THE BETTER THE VINEGAR THE MORE FLAVOR)

⅓ CUP EXTRA VIRGIN OLIVE OIL

3 SPRIGS BASIL

BREADROLLS

4 ⅔ CUPS BREAD FLOUR

1 TEASPOON WHITE SUGAR

⅕ OUNCE FINE SEA SALT

1 ½ TABLESPOONS BUTTER

½ OUNCE DRIED ACTIVE YEAST

TO ASSEMBLE

2 BALLS BUFFALO MOZZARELLA, ABOUT 4 OUNCES EACH, SLICED

16 BASIL LEAVES

SEA SALT AND FRESHLY GROUND BLACK PEPPER

For the eggplant, lay the slices in a heatproof tray, sprinkle with the salt and let stand for 5 minutes, then rinse off the salt and pat dry with a paper towel. Heat a cast-iron chargrill (griddle) pan or skillet over high heat. Brush one side of the eggplant slices with the olive oil, place oiled side down in the pan and seal until lightly browned. Remove from the pan and lay back on the tray in a single layer.

Place the garlic, vinegar and extra virgin olive oil in a saucepan and bring to a boil, then pour over the eggplant, add the basil sprigs and allow to cool. The liquid mixture should cover the eggplant completely.

For the breadrolls, place the flour, sugar and salt in a large bowl. Heat a generous cup of water and the butter in a small saucepan over low heat until the butter has just melted, then take off the heat and let stand until you can comfortably put your finger in it. Add the yeast and whisk until fully dissolved, then add to the flour mixture and mix until a smooth dough forms. Cover with a tea towel and leave to prove in a warm place for 30–40 minutes or until the dough has doubled in size.

Preheat the oven to 400°F. Lightly flour a large baking sheet.

Scrape out the dough onto a lightly floured work surface and punch down for 2–3 minutes to knock out all the air. Divide the bread dough into 8 small even pieces or 4 larger pieces, then roll in one hand in a circular fashion, using the bench to help create a rough ball-like figure. Place onto the floured tray and repeat with the remaining dough, spacing the balls on the tray at least 1 ¼ inches apart. Cover with the tea towel and leave to prove for 15–25 minutes or until doubled in size. Sift a little flour over the rolls and bake for 7 minutes, then remove the tray from the oven, sprinkle the rolls with a little water, return to the oven and bake for a further 20–25 minutes (a little longer for the larger rolls). To check if the rolls are ready, tap the base and you should hear a faint hollow sound. Once cooked, place onto a wire rack to cool. These breadrolls should be soft, fluffy and moist on the inside with a slightly hard crust.

To assemble—well, it seems ridiculous telling you how to make a sandwich—layer the eggplant, mozzarella and basil and season to your liking.

BRAISED EGGPLANT, TOMATO & MEATBALLS

SERVES 4 / MAKES 18 MEATBALLS

I would recommend that you serve a small portion of cooked polenta, rice or mashed potato as a side with this dish and maybe a simple leaf salad too.

MEATBALLS

1 POUND 3 OUNCES GROUND BEEF

1 FREE-RANGE OR ORGANIC EGG

½ RED ONION, FINELY DICED

3 GARLIC CLOVES, FINELY CRUSHED

FINE SEA SALT AND FRESHLY GROUND BLACK PEPPER

5 SPRIGS THYME, LEAVES PICKED AND CHOPPED

5 SPRIGS OREGANO, LEAVES PICKED AND CHOPPED

2 TABLESPOONS SALTED BABY CAPERS, RINSED AND CHOPPED

8-12 ANCHOVY FILLETS, CHOPPED

3 TABLESPOONS OLIVE OIL

1 TABLESPOON BALSAMIC VINEGAR

2 TABLESPOONS POLENTA

BRAISE

⅓ CUP OLIVE OIL

1 LARGE EGGPLANT, CUT INTO 8 WEDGES AND SALTED FOR 5 MINUTES, THEN PATTED DRY WITH A PAPER TOWEL

1 LARGE RED ONION, SLICED

ABOUT 16 CHERRY TOMATOES, HALVED

1 TABLESPOON SUPERFINE SUGAR

⅓ CUP RED WINE VINEGAR

14 OUNCES CANNED CHOPPED TOMATOES

1 LARGE HANDFUL OF BASIL LEAVES, SHREDDED

FINELY GRATED PARMESAN, TO SERVE

For the meatballs, place all the ingredients, except the polenta, in a large bowl and beat quite hard using a massaging action with your hands until the mixture comes together and all the ingredients are distributed evenly throughout. Now mix in the polenta. Take about 1¼–1½ ounces of meat in your hands, roll into a ball and place on a tray. Take each meatball and very roughly throw between your hands to tenderize the meat, then reroll into neat balls. This also helps them keep their shape during the cooking process. Place back on the tray.

For the braise, heat 3 tablespoons of the olive oil in a large saucepan (measuring about 12 inches in diameter by 6 inches deep) over medium heat. Add nine of the meatballs and sauté for about 30 seconds each side till browned. Place the meatballs on a plate for later. Repeat with the remaining meatballs.

Add a generous tablespoon of olive oil to the same pan, add half of the eggplant and pan fry. Remove from the pan, place on a different plate and reserve for later. Repeat with the remaining olive oil and eggplant.

Keep the heat consistent all the time to retain heat in the saucepan.

Add the onion to the same pan and sweat down a little until soft. Add the halved tomatoes and cook out a little for 4 minutes. Now add the sugar and vinegar and deglaze the pan.

Add the canned tomatoes and ¾ cup of water and bring to a boil. Add the eggplant, cover with a lid, turn the heat down to a simmer and cook for 10–12 minutes.

Add the meatballs and carefully stir them into the sauce. Turn the heat down to low, cover again and cook for 10 minutes. To serve, scatter over the basil and Parmesan and place the pan in the middle of the table with a large serving spoon.

SPICY EGGPLANT BRAISE

*The spices in this dish really bring out the flavors of the eggplant. I use this as a base
for all sorts of things, but it's a must-try as a sauce for pasta or as a side to chicken or veal.*

2 EGGPLANTS (I PREFER PURPLE ONES),
CUT INTO ¾–1¼ INCH CUBES

2 TABLESPOONS FINE SEA SALT

1 CUP OLIVE OIL

2 RED ONIONS, DICED

1 GARLIC CLOVE, CRUSHED

1 TEASPOON CUMIN SEEDS

½ TEASPOON GROUND TURMERIC

½ TEASPOON SWEET PAPRIKA

1 PINCH OF CAYENNE PEPPER

2 TOMATOES, DICED

1 TABLESPOON SUPERFINE SUGAR

JUICE OF 1 LEMON

2 TABLESPOONS CHOPPED
ITALIAN PARSLEY

Place the eggplant in a bowl, sprinkle with the salt and leave for 20 minutes, then rinse off the salt and pat dry with a paper towel. Heat a large skillet over medium–high heat, add half of the olive oil, then the eggplant and sauté until golden brown all over. Remove from the pan and set aside for later. You may need to do this in two batches.

Wipe out the pan, return to low heat, add the remaining olive oil, then the onion and garlic and cook until soft. Add the spices and cook out for 3 minutes. Add the eggplant back to the pan along with the tomato, sugar, lemon juice and ⅔ cup of water and cook for 5–7 minutes. Take off the heat, check the seasoning, then stir in the parsley. Enjoy straight away or it will keep for up to 4 days in the fridge.

VITAMIN C

ANCIENT PLANT FROM COASTAL MEDITERRANEAN.
ROMANS USED WIDELY AS FOOD & MEDICINE

Grows over 6 feet 7 inches tall:
GROWS EASILY FROM SEED

Aniseed flavor comes from
aromatic compound - Anithole

FENNEL

member of the parsley family

FENNEL

*Fennel, like cilantro and beets, is a true multi-purpose plant. You can use all of the plant,
from the seed and the frond (which is another term for the leaf) to the bulb itself.*

WILD BEAUTY

Fennel is not what I would term a "universal"
plant, meaning you won't find it being used
the whole world over, but it has crossed many
European borders. To me, it is a European
vegetable. In colder climes, the fennel seed is
used a lot for curing and in braises and sausages.
Florence fennel is the most common to grow.
It's a very beautiful plant, quite ornamental and
often grown for beauty's sake alone, regardless
of its edibility.

If you think you have never seen a fennel plant
growing before, you are probably wrong. Stick
it in the ground and it grows, pretty much
anywhere. Fennel is all around you, though you
probably just haven't realized. It grows wild and
if you pay attention the next time you're on
the train, you'll see lots of wild fennel out the
window and along many highway embankments.
They grow quite tall (around shoulder height
if left to their own devices) and have beautiful
small edible yellow flowers. The bulbs of the wild
variety tend to be fibrous and quite inedible. I
wouldn't recommend trying it.

USES

Fennel has been used and grown for millennia,
traditionally as a medicinal herb. Perhaps, most
famously, it is credited with assisting in giving
mankind the gift of fire. According to ancient
Greek mythology, Prometheus, a Titan, stole fire
from Zeus, the King of the Gods, and hid it in
a fennel stalk to bring it to earth and give it to
mankind. Pliny the Elder, the ancient Roman
historian, discussed fennel's use in his famous
encyclopaedic work, *Naturaliz Historia*, in which
he listed at least 20 diseases that fennel was
commonly thought to aid in treating. Indeed,
it has been used for centuries as a digestive aid,
appetite suppressant and weight-loss agent.
Crushed seed or leaf can be steeped in hot water
to make a lovely tea, and it's in this form that
it's supposed to aid digestion. On traditional
fasting days or during long church sermons,
people chewed on fennel seeds to quiet a hungry
stomach.

GROWING

Last year was the first time I tried to grow fennel
myself, and sadly I wasn't very successful, only
managing small bulbs, which I pulled out and
ate as babies. They were quite tasty. Hopefully

I'll have more success this year. It really is quite foreign to me to grow fennel. On a recent trip to Italy, I remember looking across at this vast green field and thinking it looked like a marsh. On closer inspection I saw that it was in fact a field of fennel. All the fronds were swaying in the breeze and looked almost like a green mist. It was really quite amazing and very beautiful.

COOKING

Fennel is as delicious raw as it is cooked and it has a wonderful fresh aniseed and menthol bite. It tastes of licorice and anise, but then it is also unlike both of them, being much more delicate in flavor. It's great with any heavy dishes to lighten them and give balance. Slow-cooked or braised dishes that are quite fatty, such as pork belly, goat neck (see page 140), and lamb shoulder or neck, need clean flavors like fennel to cut through the fat.

One tip to really enhance the lovely delicate flavor of fennel is to cook it with a dash of Pernod, the lovely French apéritif made from star anise and fennel extract. It will really lift your dish.

Fennel is also a beautiful match to fish. Its delightful herbaceous aniseed notes sit so well with fish and it is a classic vegetable used in escabeche and curing of fishes (see page 139). Escabeche is a traditional method of pickling fried (or sometimes poached) seafood, which is used all over the Mediterranean, where the fish is placed in a heavily acidic marinade. It is oh-so delicious. I really can't stress enough how fine a match fennel and fish are.

Elizabeth Schneider says in her book *Uncommon Fruits & Vegetables*: "In culinary terms fennel means Italy," where they love fennel so much they serve it in every dish from canapés right through to desserts. If you have never thought of eating sweetened fennel, then you should definitely try

the recipe I have included for frozen vanilla syrup-coated fennel (see page 143). You may think this sounds a little odd, but trust me—as a little sweet or palate cleanser between dishes, it is lovely. It will freshen your mouth in readiness for the next course. In India, sugared fennel seeds are often chewed after a meal to sweeten the breath and aid in the digestion of the food.

Is there anything fennel can't do? Eat it from root to tip. Consume it with both sweet and savory dishes. Combine it with meat or fish. It is a truly delightful, delicate vegetable that I really love.

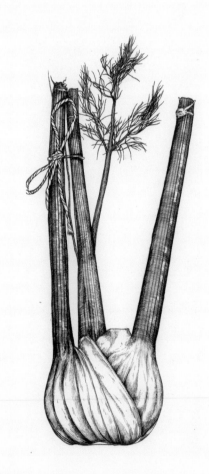

BAKED FENNEL, BREAD CRUMBS & HERBS, WITH OR WITHOUT ANCHOVY

SERVES 4

A perfect side for all things. It doesn't have to have the anchovy if it doesn't take your fancy, but I just love the balance of flavor it brings to the dish.

3 ½ OUNCES FRESH CIABATTA, TORN INTO PINKY-NAIL-SIZED BITS

⅓ CUP OLIVE OIL

2 LARGE FENNEL

1 ½ TABLESPOONS BUTTER

3 TABLESPOONS CHOPPED THYME

3 TABLESPOONS CHOPPED ITALIAN PARSLEY

12–16 ANCHOVY FILLETS (OR NOT)

SEA SALT AND FRESHLY GROUND BLACK PEPPER

Preheat the oven to 400°F. Place the bread crumbs on a large baking sheet and toss with 3 teaspoons of the olive oil. Bake for 8 minutes or until semi-crisp. Take out and set aside for later.

Cut the fennel in half from the root to the top, then cut each half into four wedges. Heat a 10 inch skillet over high heat, add 3 tablespoons of the olive oil, then add the fennel and brown slightly on one side. Once browned, add ⅓ cup of water and the butter and cook out for 3 minutes or until the liquid has reduced by half. Pour into a cast-iron baking dish (measuring 8½ x 6 x 1½ inches), scatter over the herbs, place the anchovies over the top, scatter over the bread crumbs, drizzle with the remaining oil, season with salt and pepper and bake for about 25 minutes. It's ready when the fennel can be easily pierced with a fork.

FENNEL-CURED SALMON
WITH ESCABECHE VEGETABLES

This is one of my all-time favorite dishes. My salmon of choice is New Zealand regal salmon, a Chinook breed originally from the North Pacific Ocean, now farmed in the Marlborough Sounds region. You can use any oily fish but remember the curing time will vary. Try it with kingfish, sardines or even anchovies. I like to do this amount for two and eat a little over a few days.

CURED SALMON

2 POUNDS 4 OUNCES SIDE OF SALMON
WITH SKIN ON (SEE NOTE)

½ CUP SEA SALT

⅓ CUP WHITE SUGAR

1 TABLESPOON FENNEL SEEDS, TOASTED
AND ROUGHLY CRUSHED

2 ¾ OUNCES FENNEL, FRONDS RESERVED,
AND BULBS BRUISED WITH A CLEAVER

FINELY GRATED ZEST OF 1 LEMON

ESCABECHE VEGETABLES

4 SHALLOTS, SLICED

4 BABY CARROTS, THINLY SLICED INTO ROUNDS

1 FENNEL, FRONDS RESERVED AND BULBS SHAVED

3 GARLIC CLOVES, THINLY SLICED

GOOD PINCH FINE SEA SALT

15 TURNS OF WHITE PEPPER FROM A MILL

2 TEASPOONS CORIANDER SEEDS,
TOASTED AND ROUGHLY CRUSHED

⅓ CUP RED WINE VINEGAR

1 ¼ CUPS EXTRA VIRGIN OLIVE OIL

1 ¼ CUPS WHITE WINE (TRY A RIESLING)

½ CUP FINELY CHOPPED MIXED HERBS
(I RECOMMEND DILL, PARSLEY AND CHERVIL)

HORSERADISH CREAM (SEE PAGE 165), TO SERVE

For the escabeche vegetables, place the vegetables, salt, pepper and crushed coriander seed in a large heatproof bowl, toss to coat and leave to sit for 5 minutes. Put the vinegar, oil and wine in a saucepan and bring to a boil. Take off the heat, pour over the vegetables and allow to cool.

For the cured salmon, place the salmon skin side down in a tray that is at least 1¼ inches deep. Mix the remaining ingredients together, including the reserved fennel fronds, and pat onto the salmon. Leave to cure for 12 hours in the fridge. Rinse the salmon thoroughly and pat dry with a paper towel. Place the salmon skin side down on a chopping board and cut into ¹⁄₁₆ inch thick slices, making sure to not cut through the skin—the salmon flesh should come away from the skin easily. Arrange the slices on a plate. Stir the herbs into the escabeche vegetables, then spoon over the fish. Serve with the horseradish cream.

Note Ask your fishmonger to remove the belly fat and pin-bone the salmon. Ensure you have exactly 2 pounds 4 ounces of the fish with the skin on. The total weight before this should be around 3 pounds 2 ounces.

SHAVED FENNEL & MOZZARELLA SALAD WITH BRAISED GOAT NECK

SERVES 4–6

This salad by itself is amazing. It's just so fresh and cuts through any dish with a high fat content that coats the palate. The sweet and sour goat is a winner, too—try it with polenta or cooked green beans.

BRAISED GOAT NECK

3 TABLESPOONS OLIVE OIL

2 GOAT NECKS (2 POUNDS 10 OUNCES–3 POUNDS 2 OUNCES TOTAL)

1 CARROT, CUT INTO 4 PIECES

1 ONION

2 STICKS CELERY, CUT INTO 3 PIECES EACH

5 GARLIC CLOVES, ROUGHLY CHOPPED

¼ BUNCH OF THYME

1 TEASPOON EACH OF SMOKED PAPRIKA, GROUND CUMIN, GROUND CINNAMON, GROUND CORIANDER

¼ TEASPOON GROUND CARDAMON

1 ¼ CUPS APPLE CIDER VINEGAR

⅔ CUP UNREFINED LIGHT BROWN SUGAR

14 OUNCES CANNED WHOLE TOMATOES

2 TEASPOONS FINE SEA SALT

FENNEL SALAD

1 LARGE FENNEL OR 2 SMALL, THINLY SLICED ON A MANDOLINE

2 BALLS BUFFALO MOZZARELLA, ABOUT 4 OUNCES EACH, TORN INTO CHUNKS

½ BUNCH ITALIAN PARSLEY, LEAVES PICKED AND ROUGHLY TORN

3 TABLESPOONS ORGANIC RAW ALMONDS, SLICED

SEA SALT AND FRESHLY GROUND PEPPER

PRESERVED LEMON DRESSING (SEE PAGE 275)

For the braised goat neck, heat the olive oil in a 12-cup capacity saucepan over high heat, add the goat necks and sear all over until colored. Remove from the pan, turn down the heat to medium, then add the carrot, onion, celery and garlic and cook until colored. Add the thyme and spices and cook out for 3 minutes. Add the vinegar and sugar and cook until reduced by half. Add the goat necks back to the pan along with the tomatoes, salt and enough water to cover the necks, bring to a boil, then turn down the heat to a simmer, cover with a lid and cook for 3 hours or until the meat is tender.

For the fennel salad, the most important thing to keep in mind is the freshness of it. You can prepare all the ingredients ahead of time (keep the shaved fennel in acidulated water), but dress the salad at the last minute.

Once the goat neck is cooked, remove the meat from the pan, pick the meat off the bones and keep warm. Pass the cooking liquid through a strainer and discard the solids. Add the picked goat meat to the sauce.

Mix all the salad ingredients, reserving a little mozzarella, parsley and almonds to garnish. Dress the salad with just enough dressing to coat and garnish with the reserved bits. Serve with the goat.

FROZEN VANILLA SYRUP-COATED FENNEL

SERVES AS MANY AS YOU LIKE

Something that has seemed to die in restaurants over the past decade is the once-great palate cleanser served before or after mains. This would be in the form of a sherbet, salad or even a refreshing clear cold tomato soup. You could serve this as either a simple palate cleanser or you could use it as a garnish for a chocolate dessert.

VANILLA SYRUP

¾ CUP SUPERFINE SUGAR

½ VANILLA BEAN, SPLIT AND SEEDS SCRAPED

1 MEDIUM FENNEL

To make the vanilla syrup, place the sugar, vanilla bean and seeds and ²/₃ cup of water in a saucepan and bring to a boil over medium heat, then pour into a container and chill in the fridge.

Line a tray that will fit in your freezer with parchment paper. Thinly slice the fennel on a mandoline from the root to tip so you get a full cross-section of the fennel. Take the syrup out of the fridge and submerge the fennel in the vanilla syrup. Remove the fennel, shaking each slice to remove the excess syrup and place on the tray in a single layer. When the first layer is complete, lay a sheet of parchment paper on top and keep layering until all the fennel is in the tray. Place in the freezer for about 2 hours or until frozen.

When you're ready to serve, remove from the freezer, place onto the desired plate and serve immediately. The fennel should be cold, crisp and have a taste of aniseed with a sweetened vanilla aroma.

FOLKLORE REPUTATION

Prevents everything from
common cold to PLAGUE

allicin & dicillyt sulphides

Has been cultivated as food & medicine
for thousands of years - thought to have
come from mountains of Central Asia

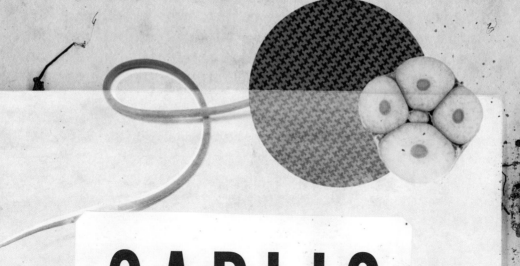

GARLIC

MEMBER OF THE LILY FAMILY.

GARLIC

Garlic is the most maligned foodstuff I can think of, with probably the worst reputation from being cooked poorly and without respect.

NATURE'S ANTIBIOTIC

Humans have used garlic for thousands of years in food and medicine and praised it, both for its beautiful flavor and its antibiotic properties. Islamic myth has it that the garlic plant sprang up in Satan's left footprint as he was driven out of Eden. The ancient Egyptians thought it so powerful that they buried their dead with it. There are myths and magic surrounding garlic the whole world over and, depending on whom you believe, it's native to either Asia or the Mediterranean or Africa. Well, I guess people will fight over its origin because it is central to cuisines the world over. What is a stir-fry without garlic? Or Bolognese? Or curry?

BUY THE BEST THERE IS

It's available in just about every form, be it fresh, freeze-dried, as a paste, in powder form and granulated (but just don't buy the pre-minced garlic in a jar). My rule of thumb is simple: buy the best garlic there is on offer. For example, there's garlic that's $7.99 per kilogram and garlic that's $39.99 per kilogram, side by side at the grocer. You only need one bulb—even if you cook with garlic every day, and that one bulb will last you a week. Even if it cost you $1.20 compared to 40 cents, that 80 cents difference will give you 80 per cent difference in

flavor and quality of not only the garlic but any dish you put it in. It's also an investment—good garlic will last four months, stored in a dry cool place.

GROWING

Most people probably wouldn't think of growing their own garlic, but it is one of the easiest and loveliest things to grow. I only really got to know about techniques for growing garlic in the past two years through meeting people, including Brendan at Daylesford Organics and more recently Tim from Angelica Organic Farm, at farmers' markets, and I thought about having a go at growing it myself. It's amazing. Put one clove in the ground and, almost miraculously, a green shoot will appear. Over the next six months, the shoot produces a beautiful purple, blue or white blossom, depending on which variety you have. Then the shoot dies, which is the sign for you to dig down from a clove and you'll discover a new bulb. Within that bulb there is a little shoot in the middle. Store that in a cool dark place until it has dried out, then replant and, from that single clove of garlic, another bulb will emerge.

Another way to grow garlic is to save the seed when the plant flowers, then sow it. Interestingly, though, from the seed, only an individual clove of garlic will grow—this is fittingly dubbed single clove garlic or sweet garlic, which is highly sought after and absolutely stunning. Garlic has a much more refined flavor when grown as a single clove. Just finely chop and fry the single clove, or even just poach it whole in milk, and taste the flavor difference for yourself.

You'll notice if you grow it yourself that garlic can reproduce in all sorts of different shapes and sizes, which makes it all the more amazing that organic growers can consistently produce beautiful uniform cloves and heads.

When I was young I'd pick wild garlic that grew all around the creeks in Barnsley and around Silkston. Twice a year it would come up and flower, but it was always strongest in spring, and I always remember walking the dog or going on horse treks with my sister and having the smell of sweet garlic in the breeze. You could simply pick the gorgeous green stalks and bite them. The taste was so fresh, mild and beautiful.

VARIETIES

There are about 600 cultivated varieties, though we are rarely offered so many at the supermarket. If you want to try some different kinds then I'd suggest either going to a farmers' market or good organic grocer where they may stock a few different types. They are often named after their place of origin, like Australian White, New Zealand Purple and Italian White and, when you're cooking garlic, it does pay to be aware of the different varieties and flavors available, from really earthy hazelnut flavors to really sweet, almost vinegar-scented ones. Sometimes garlic can even be almost reminiscent of ginger and galangal.

PREPARATION AND COOKING

If you use lovely fresh garlic, it should be quite mild. To check if the garlic is fresh, cut a clove in half and if there is a green shoot inside, it means that it is getting old (and basically is ready to be planted again). Ideally you can save the entire clove and plant it. You can use the clove in your cooking but make sure you remove the green shoot first as it's quite indigestible and, more importantly, it has a different, more astringent and entirely unpleasant, flavor to the rest of the garlic.

Should you find that your garlic is very strong smelling and almost "sappy" on your fingers when you're peeling it, then it is best to blanch it to get rid of some of the excess oil. Take peeled whole cloves (or halved with the green shoot removed if necessary), put in a saucepan and cover with cold water with a pinch of salt and bring to a boil, then drain. Repeat the processs with fresh cold salted water four more times to remove the sappy residue and the "garlicky" aftertaste.

Garlic needs to be cooked; if you eat it raw or add it to a dish at the last minute, you can't maximize on its full sweetness and flavor potential.

I've heard some top chefs say you shouldn't toast garlic or let it go crispy—but I love crisp brown garlic! Especially in pasta with some fresh anchovies, tomatoes and herbs.

Garlic benefits from being braised, say, in a beef stew. Halve the garlic first so they take on the rich beef flavors. Another lovely and easy thing to do is to simply poach potatoes and a heap of garlic cloves in milk. Just bring the mixture up to a simmer and cook until the potatoes are soft. Season, throw the mix in a blender and you have a beautiful soup that you can serve with toasted garlic as a garnish. This is a delicate soup to which you can add croûtons, lardons or broiled sardines.

Everyone gets scared of stinking like garlic. But if you treat it properly you shouldn't wake up in the morning with a garlic hangover.

BAGNA CÀUDA WITH PIEDMONTESE GARNISHES

SERVES 2 (OR 8 AS A NIBBLE)

Recently while in Piedmont in Italy I had this most beautiful dip called bagna càuda with raw and roasted vegetables as garnishes as a snack. Bagna càuda is a garlic and anchovy sauce, which not only works superbly with chicken and any game birds but is also lovely smeared on bread with some lettuce and slices of hot beef.

BAGNA CÀUDA

15 LARGE GARLIC CLOVES, SLICED INTO FOUR

⅔ CUP MILK

⅓ CUP EXTRA VIRGIN OLIVE OIL

3 TABLESPOONS CHARDONNAY VINEGAR

1 LONG RED CHILI, HALVED, SEEDS REMOVED AND THINLY SLICED

1 TEASPOON WHITE SUGAR

10 ANCHOVY FILLETS

FINE SEA SALT

PIEDMONTESE GARNISHES

THE CLASSIC GARNISHES OF THE OLD PIEDMONTESE DAYS ARE COOKED CARDOON STALK AND RAW RED PEPPER, BUT I LIKE TO USE A SELECTION OF THE FOLLOWING:

THINLY SLICED RAW SUNCHOKES

HALVED RAW RADISHES

ROMAINE LETTUCE LEAVES AND HEARTS

RADICCHIO LEAVES

RED BELGIAN ENDIVE LEAVES

RAW BABY TURNIPS

CABBAGE LEAVES

BABY CARROTS

ROASTED PEPPERS (SEE PAGE 73)

ROASTED BEETS (SEE PAGE 32)

CELERY STICKS

CRUSTY FRESH BREAD

For the bagna càuda, place the garlic and milk in a saucepan and bring to a boil, turn down the heat to low and gently simmer for 10–15 minutes or until the garlic has softened. Strain, discarding the milk. Give the garlic a rinse and pat dry with paper towels. Wash out the pan and return the garlic to it. Add the olive oil and cook over low heat for 40–50 minutes or until the garlic starts to turn a light brown but make sure it does not catch on the base of the pan. Now add the vinegar, chili and sugar and cook for 10–15 minutes or until the chili softens. Add the anchovies and cook for 4–5 minutes. Take off the heat and, using a fork, mash all the ingredients together until mushy. Taste to see if it needs some salt and maybe a little more vinegar. Serve warm with your desired garnishes.

GREEN GARLIC CHAMP
WITH POACHED EGG & BROILED OX TONGUE

SERVES 4 AS AN ENTRÉE

Green garlic is immature garlic and is a lot like scallions—
you can use the top and the bulb part of the plant. You may turn your nose up
at ox tongue but I love it and any good butcher should have some.

GREEN GARLIC CHAMP

2 CUPS MILK

5½ OUNCES CHOPPED GREEN GARLIC (YOUNG SINGLE CLOVE GARLIC), GREEN TIPS RESERVED

1 POTATO (A GOOD MASHING VARIETY), SLICED

SEA SALT

JUICE OF 1 LEMON

3 TEASPOONS WHITE VINEGAR

4 FREE-RANGE OR ORGANIC EGGS

8 SLICES PICKLED OX TONGUE FROM YOUR LOCAL BUTCHER

¼ BUNCH ITALIAN PARSLEY, LEAVES PICKED AND CHOPPED

For the green garlic champ, place the milk in a 6-cup capacity saucepan and bring to a boil, whisking all the time to prevent scorching on the base. Add the garlic and potato and cook for 15 minutes or until they are soft. Pass through a strainer, reserving both the cooking liquid and solids. Blitz the solids in a food processor, adding a little bit of the reserved cooking liquid at a time until the mixture is the consistency of wet polenta. Season with the salt and lemon juice to taste and stir through the green tips of the garlic.

For the poached eggs, place 4 cups of water and the vinegar in a 8-cup capacity saucepan, bring to a boil, then turn down the heat to a simmer. With a spoon, stir the water counter-clockwise, then crack in all four eggs. Poach for 3–3½ minutes or until the whites are cooked but the yolks still oozy. Remove with a slotted spoon, pat dry on a tea towel and, kapow, you've got yourself a perfect runny poached egg.

Heat a chargrill (griddle) pan over medium–high heat and broil the ox tongue on both sides.

To serve, place some of the garlic champ on each plate, lay a slice of tongue over, top with a poached egg and sprinkle with the parsley. I'd even add some of the lightly pickled shallots from page 201.

SMOKED & BAKED GARLIC
WITH A SIMPLE GOOD OLD ROAST CHICKEN

SERVES 4

My friends Meg and Blakey have a farm down in the Grampians in Victoria, Australia, and they produce the most beautiful smoked garlic which they sell at farmers' markets. This is an accompaniment to a roasted free-range chicken and is one of the highlights of simple cookery to me.

4 SMALL BULBS OF ORGANIC GARLIC

1 CUP SMOKING CHIPS (FOUND AT MOST HOME AND HARDWARE STORES)

½ BUNCH THYME

½ BUNCH OREGANO

½ CUP JASMINE RICE

4 POUNDS FREE-RANGE CHICKEN

⅓ CUP OLIVE OIL

SEA SALT AND FRESHLY GROUND BLACK PEPPER

Preheat the oven to 500°F and arrange two racks inside.

Soak the bulbs of garlic in water for 5 minutes or so. This helps the smoke absorb into the garlic and it also prevents it from burning.

Line a heavy-bottomed flameproof roasting tray (measuring 11½ x 11½ x 2 inches) with foil. Place the smoking chips, herbs and rice into the tray and place over low heat. Place a wire rack inside the tray over the smoking chip mixture and sit the bulbs of garlic on the rack. When the chips start to change color to a light brown, cover the tray with foil and place in the oven.

Take another roasting tray of similar size. Rinse the chicken inside and out with water and pat dry with paper towels. Place the chicken in the tray, rub all over with the olive oil and season with the salt. Roast for 25 minutes, then turn down the heat to 350°F and continue roasting for a further 20 minutes. Take the chicken and garlic out of the oven. Slice the chicken in between the leg and body and if there are no pink bits in between the leg and thigh bones, then it is cooked. Leave the chicken on top of the stove for 15 minutes to rest.

Carve the chicken into pieces and place the smoked garlic alongside. The smoked garlic should be a beautiful dark brown. Let your guests pod the garlic out of its skin and eat whole. It's a whole new experience eating garlic this way. I'd serve this dish with a simple salad of leaves from the garden (see page 172) or any other vegetables that are in season.

grows well in a deep container
or an old bucket in the ground
to prevent spreading

HARVEST
IN 16-24 WEEKS

Man's use of horseradish dates back as far as man himself. The ancient Greeks believed in its healing properties for tired muscles.

It grows up to 5 feet tall. The Japanese call it the Western world's wasabi.

HORSERADISH

HORSERADISH IS AN AGGRESSIVE GROWER AND WILL QUICKLY TAKE OVER THE GARDEN

HORSERADISH

Horseradish packs the most amazing flavor punch and, although it's thought to have originated in central Europe, to me, it is the quintessential British vegetable. Some people argue it's not a vegetable but more a spice or accompaniment, but it is my true love, and a complement for everything.

WHAT'S IN A NAME?

Well, one story is that the name horseradish comes from the Germans, who call it "meerrettich" or sea radish as it grows near the sea. Somewhere along the line the English began to mispronounce it as "mare-radish" and from there it wasn't much of a stretch to horseradish.

Man's use of horseradish dates about as far back as man himself. The ancient Greeks believed in its healing properties for tired muscles, and it is central to the celebration of Passover for Jewish people, being listed as one of the "five bitter herbs" they are instructed to eat during this holy time, along with cilantro, romaine lettuce, horehound and nettles. The Japanese call it the Western world's wasabi, and they're not far wrong as it is a relative of both wasabi and mustard, which is where it gets its vicious, delicious bite from.

THE ULTIMATE ACCOMPANIMENT

Horseradish's best match has to be beef. Beef without horseradish is like Romeo without Juliet. The two are just meant to be together, married

forever. It's not as suited to other meats, although it can add a nice heat and sweetness to sauces and gravies. Where it really shines is with fish and vegetables. It's beautiful with parsnip, sharing that same mustard flavor. It's traditionally served in Russia and Eastern Europe with beets and enhances the natural sweetness of turnips and carrots. I think it's a highly underrated accompaniment for other vegetables. Its classic use in Scandinavia is to cure salmon and white cod, and it is highly complementary to any cured fish. Horseradish crème fraîche or just fresh horseradish grated over right before serving is amazing.

Its leaves are often overlooked for culinary use, but you can use them as you would any mustardy leaf. You may think that the flavor would be too intense because of the heat, but it's really lovely. Use them sautéed and served on their own as an accompaniment or add at the last minute to Asian dishes.

GROWING

Horseradish is a root vegetable, like carrot, beets and parsnip, and is what's known as a rhizome, which means that it produces roots that stretch out horizontally. When you pull the plant from the ground, these roots snap off and remain, continuing to grow and eventually producing another horseradish plant. Ginger and sunchokes reproduce in the same way. It's a delicate process, and this is why most of the world's horseradish crop is still harvested by hand.

You should be able to find fresh horseradish all year round, though it does better in the colder weather than warm. It's not a big fan of summer and struggles a bit. When growing, it does need quite a bit of water but it is still quite a hardy plant. When you're growing your own, let it get to the size of a small parsnip before harvesting.

USING

The recipes included here use what seems like quite a lot of horseradish. To use fresh horseradish, simply use a vegetable peeler to remove the skin from a small section. For the best result, only peel as much as you need to use, as this will help the horseradish to keep for up to a week. Use a Microplane (or fine grater) and grate the horseradish over the top of the dish immediately before serving.

One word of warning when grating fresh horseradish: I would highly recommend wearing gloves. And goggles. Even swimming goggles. You may feel a bit of a fool, but it'll save you plenty of tears. At one of my first jobs at Warren House in London, my head chef, Mike Taylor, made me grate about a kilo of fresh horseradish. It was ten times worse than chopping onions. My mouth and nostrils were burning. Tears were streaming down my face. Unbeknown to me, he stood behind a curtain laughing at me! I managed to grate it all, but it wasn't very pleasant.

Another tip is if you realize you have too big a root and you won't be able to use it before it's past its best, cut it into small pieces, wrap it in foil and freeze. Thaw as you need and use as you would the fresh stuff. Otherwise, I am not opposed to a jar of good-quality pre-prepared horseradish. I know it seems controversial to say, but you have to think that these products were preserved in their prime, so I'd always choose the product that is of better quality and has better flavor. Sometimes this can be the canned, frozen or preserved version. I prefer to use something that has been captured at the peak of its season than to make do with the fresh version that is either out of season or past its best (I elaborate more on this in the tomato chapter on pages 250–63). When deciding which canned or pre-prepared variety to choose, my rule of thumb is to look at the list of ingredients on the side and choose the one with the least ingredients (for example, only horseradish, vinegar, salt and sugar), the one with the highest percentage of horseradish and without any preservatives as the vinegar is the preservative. It really shouldn't need any chemicals added.

I've included the recipe for my nan's roast beef with Yorkshire pudding (see page 165), and I insist that you make the horseradish cream that goes with it.

HORSERADISH & CELERIAC SALAD WITH SUGAR & SALT CURED BEEF

SERVES 4

This salad is simply a rémoulade. You've probably seen it somewhere before, but here I've combined the earthy/peppery taste of the horseradish, the earthy sweetness of the celeriac and the freshness of the apple to make a mesmerising dish, great with not only cured meats but also most seafood and chicken.

SUGAR & SALT CURED BEEF

1 CUP SEA SALT

½ CUP UNREFINED LIGHT BROWN SUGAR

½ TEASPOON SICHUAN PEPPERCORNS

2 ALLSPICE BERRIES

1 STAR ANISE

6 JUNIPER BERRIES

1 POUND BEEF RUMP CAP, TRIMMED OF ALL FAT
(ASK YOUR BUTCHER TO DO THIS FOR YOU)

SALAD

1 CELERIAC (CELERY ROOT) (ABOUT 14 OUNCES)
(PROBABLY THE WORLD'S MOST UNDERRATED VEG)

4 SMALL APPLES (MY FAVORITE ARE
LITTLE NEW-SEASON GALA)

PINCH FINE SEA SALT

JUICE OF ½ LEMON

1 MEDIUM HANDFUL OF ITALIAN
PARSLEY LEAVES, CHOPPED

½ CUP MAYONNAISE

9 OUNCES PIECE OF FRESH HORSERADISH, PEELED

TO SERVE

EXTRA VIRGIN OLIVE OIL, FOR DRIZZLING

3 TABLESPOONS PARSLEY SHOOTS

BABY NASTURTIUM LEAVES (OPTIONAL)

BROILED SOURDOUGH AND ROMESCO
SAUCE (SEE PAGE 73) (OPTIONAL)

For the sugar and salt cured beef, place the salt, sugar and spices in a mortar and coarsely grind. Place the beef on a tray, sprinkle over the salt cure and roll to coat well. Cover and refrigerate for 2 hours. Remove the beef and lightly wash, then pat dry. Heat a broiler or chargrill (griddle) pan to high and char the beef all over. Alternatively, seal in a hot skillet (with no oil added). Allow to cool, then thinly slice.

For the salad, thinly slice the celeriac and apple on a mandoline, then cut into thin strips. Toss with the salt. Allow to sit for 2 minutes. Mix in the lemon juice, parsley and mayonnaise. Grate in some horseradish (about one-third, depending on how peppery you like it), reserving some to garnish.

Place the salad onto a serving dish, layer over the slices of cured beef, drizzle with olive oil, grate over some horseradish and top with the parsley shoots and nasturtium leaves. Serve with the sourdough and romesco.

HORSERADISH & TARRAGON MUSTARD

FILLS 3 STANDARD PRESERVING JARS

Sometimes what appears to be the most complicated is usually the easiest.
Our supermarket shelves have become stocked to the brim with food items that seem
too tiresome or hard to make, so we find ourselves buying these things for convenience.
Mustard is a prime example. Only a few years ago, I thought, "Mustard, geez that sounds hard
to make!" But after looking at Stephanie Alexander's recipe for grain mustard, I realized just how easy
and non-time consuming it is to make mustard—and how much better the homemade stuff tasted.
These traditional recipes and forgotten skills of cooking need preserving.
This is my recipe, honed from the many times I've made it, and I can tell you that it's a beauty.
Once you've made it, you will not look to those jars on the supermarket shelf again.

2 CUPS YELLOW AND BROWN
MUSTARD SEEDS

½ CUP HOT WATER

2½ OUNCES TARRAGON LEAVES, CHOPPED

½ CUP FINELY GRATED FRESH
PEELED HORSERADISH

2 TABLESPOONS FINE SEA SALT

1 ½ CUPS APPLE CIDER VINEGAR

Blitz 1 ¼ cups of the mustard seeds in a spice grinder until a fine powder. Tip into a large bowl, add the remaining mustard seeds and the hot water and mix. Leave to sit for 5 minutes, then whisk in the remaining ingredients.

Transfer to a non-reactive container, cover with a damp tea towel and leave at room temperature for 2 days. Give it a stir each day, then transfer to preserving jars with lids. Store for 3 weeks before using. Store opened jars in the fridge for up to 3 months. Unopened jars will keep for years.

HORSERADISH WAFERS

*A great simple snack to use as a base for a canapé or mix in with a salad
for some crunch instead of croûtons.*

¾ CUP FINELY GRATED PARMESAN

1 TABLESPOON ALL-PURPOSE FLOUR

½ TABLESPOON SESAME SEEDS

1¾ OUNCES PIECE OF FRESH HORSERADISH,
PEELED AND FINELY GRATED ON A MICROPLANE

1 TEASPOON THYME LEAVES

15 TURNS OF WHITE PEPPER IN A MILL

Preheat the oven to 325°F. Grease two baking sheets with oil and line with parchment paper, trimmed to fit exactly.

Place the Parmesan, flour, sesame seeds, horseradish, thyme and pepper in a bowl and mix together.

Take a 2 ¾ inch diameter cutter and place on one of the trays. Sprinkle the Parmesan mixture into the cutter, covering the whole surface up to $^1/_8$ inch thick. Repeat making wafers on the trays, leaving room in between each for spreading. Bake for 9–12 minutes or until golden brown (see Note). Once golden, slide the wafers off the tray and onto a surface to cool.

Store in an airtight container, layered between paper towels or parchment paper for up to 2 days.

Note The outside wafers will more than likely color up before the inside ones, so turn the tray around after 6–8 minutes and take off the outside wafers, then put the tray back in the oven so the rest can finish baking.

HORSERADISH CREAM WITH A JOINT OF BEEF & ME NAN'S YORKSHIRE PUDDINGS

SERVES 4 (WITH LEFTOVERS)

The horseradish amount you use for the cream is entirely up to you. The more you use, the hotter the cream, naturally. I like to keep some back and grate it over the whole dish at the end. Can I use pre-prepared horseradish I hear you ask? Go on then, but there ain't nothing like a fresh horseradish party.

HORSERADISH CREAM

9 OUNCES CRÈME FRAÎCHE

1 OUNCE PIECE OF FRESH HORSERADISH, PEELED AND FINELY GRATED ON A MICROPLANE

JUICE OF 1 LEMON

FINE SEA SALT AND FRESHLY GROUND BLACK PEPPER

LIGHT CREAM, FOR THINNING

A JOINT OF BEEF

4 POUNDS JOINT OF SIRLOIN

2 TABLESPOONS OLIVE OIL

SEA SALT AND FRESHLY GROUND BLACK PEPPER

ME NAN'S YORKSHIRE PUDDINGS

¾ CUP SELF-RISING FLOUR, SIFTED TWICE

½ TEASPOON FINE SEA SALT

2 FREE-RANGE OR ORGANIC EGGS

1 GENEROUS CUP MILK

⅓ CUP LARD OR BEEF FAT (OR VEGETABLE OIL IF YOU'RE THINKING ABOUT YOUR WAISTLINE)

For the horseradish cream, whisk all the ingredients together. If it seems a little dry, thin with a little cream. If it seems a little wet, hang in a coffee filter or in cheesecloth in the fridge for a few hours.

For the joint of beef, preheat the oven to 400°F. Heat a large skillet over high heat for 1 minute, then add the oil. Add the beef and seal all sides. This should take 8 minutes or so. Once all the sides are browned, sit the beef on a wire rack placed inside a roasting tray. Season all sides with salt and pepper, then roast for 45–50 minutes for medium-rare. Take the beef out of the oven and check if it's cooked. Insert a metal skewer into the fattest part of the meat, then remove and run it along your bottom lip—it should feel nice and warm. Cover with foil or a heavy cloth and rest for 10 minutes. Carve into thick slices to serve.

For the Yorkshire puddings, preheat the oven to 400°F. Place the flour and salt in a bowl and make a well in the center. Add the eggs and milk and whisk until smooth. Rest for 30 minutes. Fill a 6-holed muffin tray (with holes that are at least 3¼ inches in diameter by 1¼ inches deep) with 3 teaspoons of lard in each hole and place in the oven for 15–20 minutes. This is the most crucial part to making the yorkies rise. When the lard is hot, open the oven door and spoon in the batter until it reaches almost to the brim. It's important to leave the tray in the oven so the lard doesn't lose too much heat. Bake for 15 minutes, then turn down the heat to 375°F and cook for a further 15 minutes. They should be high and golden brown. Carefully take the tray out of the oven, turn the puds out and serve straight away with the carved beef and horseradish cream on the side.

1 *Prepare horseradish cream. Season beef with salt and pepper on all sides and roast until medium rate.*

2 *Place lard or pour oil into the holes of the muffin tin and place in oven for 15-20 minutes.*

3 *When oil is hot, open oven door and spoon in the batter until just below the brim.*

4 *Continue with the remaining batter working quickly, with the oven door open so that the muffin tin and oil retain their heat.*

5 *Cook puddings for a further 15 minutes until golden brown.*

6 *Remove yorkies and serve straight away with the carved beef and horseradish cream.*

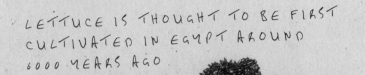

LETTUCE IS THOUGHT TO BE FIRST
CULTIVATED IN EGYPT AROUND
6000 YEARS AGO

THE DARKER THE
LETTUCE LEAF THE
MORE NUTRITIOUS
IT IS.

Silverbeet grows best in cool climates
with long hot summers
and really cold winters.

When we think of lettuce we think of
iceberg. But don't forget romaine, arugula,
English spinach, Belgian endive, mustard
greens, mache, cresses, Swiss chard, oak,
mesclun, mizuna, frisée or romaine.

LEAVES FROM
THE GARDEN

Lettuce is approximately 95% water.

LETTUCES HAVE SHALLOW ROOTS AND
THUS NEED FREQUENT WATERING

LEAVES FROM THE GARDEN

Well, I didn't want to say "salad" or "lettuce" because that would immediately limit your ideas on what you should and shouldn't use and grow, when the whole point is to open your mind right up when it comes to the beautiful and tasty things you can incorporate into your cooking.

LETTUCES, HERBS AND FLOWERS

Everyone, and I do mean everyone, can grow their own salad leaves. If you have an entire acre or just a window box, there is no excuse for not growing a few different varieties, and you'll see just how much they will enliven your salad-eating experience.

The first recipe I have included in this chapter tells you to go to your garden and pick yourself a beautiful fresh salad. But what exactly should you pick?

For example, when we think of lettuce leaf we think …What? Iceberg? Well, it's boring, but it's a start. How about romaine, arugula, English spinach, Belgian endive, mustard greens, mache, cresses, Swiss chard, oak, mesclun, mizuna, frisée or romaine? I could go on and on.

And it's not just about lettuce. How about some of the softer herbs and flowers as well? A little bit of mint or basil can really lift an arugula and red oak salad and give it a wonderful perfume. Then there are parsley and chervil, lovely little herbs with a clean, fresh flavor that complement rather than overpower other leaves. Sorrel adds a lovely lemony flavor, but it can be quite tart so use sparingly, as you would lemon juice.

If you want a splash of color, forage in your plot for some flowers. Cooking with flowers has come back into vogue of late, but it's an ancient practice that stretches back thousands of years. A fellow called John Evelyn wrote a wonderful book, in 1699, that highlights around 35 different plants, herbs and flowers that can and should be used in the making of "sallets," as they were then called. He called for the leaves of beets, celery and fennel to be utilized not just the bulbs, and he recommended a simple dressing of sweet herbaceous "oyl," finest vinegar and salt and pepper. More than 300 years after it was written, it couldn't be more relevant, and I couldn't agree with old John more.

Nasturtium flowers are a classic, and a favorite of mine, to add to salads because they are so vivid and their warm bite adds a wonderful peppery taste to a dish—not unlike watercress. But there are so many flowers you can use. Beautiful, purple borage flowers have a wonderful mild cucumber taste. Then there are pansies, violas or violets, even hibiscus and rose petals.

You can use the flowers from various herbs, too, like chive, basil, thyme, mint, sage, rosemary and marjoram. Remember, though, that the flowers will often be stronger and more pungent in flavor than the leaves, so taste first and use your judgment as to how much of these to add.

And there is one more thing that is definitely worth trying. The Italians have been onto it for aeons, and if you venture into any Italian wholesaler or butcher worth their salt, you'll find there is usually a section devoted to seeds. There'll be zucchini and herbs, lots of basil, tomatoes and more than a dozen different leaves. These are the ones I really encourage you to try. Anything from the treviso family, like Belgian endive or radicchio, in small amounts, really lifts a salad.

And don't be scared to wilt and warm salad leaves. A fellow called John Burton Race started a restaurant called L'ortolan in the UK, which went on to achieve two Michelin stars. One of the signature dishes was their salad. When a salad was ordered, he would dress it and then flash it in the oven, just for 5–10 seconds to release the flavors. The leaves were still crisp, but warmed ever so slightly. Think about the difference between eating leaves fresh from the garden, warmed by the sun when their flavor is so intense and compare that to leaves eaten cold, straight from the fridge. Try it.

And let's not forget the harder flowery herbs that can be used in all matter of things. Think beyond your usual rosemary and thyme to herbs such as pineapple sage, rose geranium and lemon verbena, all of which, fresh or dried, make a splendid herbal tea. I have included a recipe for rose-geranium-stewed blueberries with creamed rice pudding (see page 175) simply because it is delicious, and you can infuse rose geranium into a liquid to poach anything or replace it with any floral herb.

GROWING

Leaves grow all year round and are great to grow from seed. If you live in a colder climate, start them off in small seed trays. You can also buy a small hotbox to start your seeds for around $20, so

I don't want to hear anyone say they can't do it! They don't take up heaps of space and are so diverse.

In summer they will tend to bolt, as everything does with a little water and sun, but especially leaves. The term "bolt" means that the plant will use all its energy to produce flowers and seeds and reproduce itself. To prevent this, keep cutting the middle stalks. This really is worth keeping an eye on as once they have flowered they will use all their energy in growing upwards, instead of producing lovely leaves for you to eat. Don't worry about harming the plant—you won't—but if it does bolt, the new leaves will be woody and not as delicate.

HANDLING

To store your leaves don't use plastic bags as they will cause the leaves to sweat and start to break down really quickly. Wash them, then simply put into a container, covered with some damp paper towels.

Always remember to wash your greens three times. Fill two bowls with water. Drop the leaves into one, then into the other. Empty out the first bowl; refill it with clean cold water, then drop the leaves back in again. There is nothing worse than biting into a salad and getting grit between your teeth; it's nice for people to know you've grown the salad yourself, but there are far more pleasant ways to let them know than with grit.

GO STRAIGHT INTO THE GARDEN AND PICK YOUR OWN SALAD WITH HOUSE VINAIGRETTE

This is quite simply the most tastiest salad there is. Just-picked leaves, herbs and flowers that have been sun-warmed have a miraculous flavor that seems to diminish as each hour passes from the time they were picked, even faster when refrigerated. Don't despair if you don't have a garden to grow your own leaves—you can try growing a few things from the list below on your balcony or windowsill. The leaves and flowers I grow and often pick include the following.

WILD ARUGULA LEAVES AND FLOWERS

PARSLEY

PURSLANE

BASIL

CHERVIL

SNOW PEA AND PEA TENDRILS

FAVA BEAN TOPS

VIOLA AND VIOLET FLOWERS

NASTURTIUM FLOWERS AND LEAVES

MIZUNA

MACHE LETTUCE

BABY SPINACH LEAVES

BUTTER AND CORAL LETTUCES

RADICCHIO AND BITTER LEAVES LIKE TREVISO AND DANDELION

BORAGE FLOWERS

MINT

BEET TOPS

RADISH SHOOTS

MARIGOLD FLOWERS

SORREL

I like to toss the leaves lightly with my house vinaigrette on page 279, or you could try the tarragon emulsion too on page 275.

ROSE-GERANIUM-STEWED BLUEBERRIES WITH CREAMED RICE PUDDING

SERVES 6

This dish has been a favorite from the day we opened at Pope Joan. I change the fruit to whatever is in season but I always poach the fruit with a little rose geranium, which gives it such a gentle perfumed floral fragrance that works stunningly with the rich creaminess of the rice pudding.

STEWED BLUEBERRIES

1 ⅓ CUPS FRESH OR FROZEN BLUEBERRIES

½ CUP SUPERFINE SUGAR

1 LEAF AND STALK OF ROSE GERANIUM

CREAMED RICE PUDDING

⅓ CUP ARBORIO RICE

½ VANILLA BEAN (SEEDS ONLY)

2 CUPS MILK

½ CUP SUPERFINE SUGAR

½ TEASPOON GELATIN POWDER

1 CUP HEAVY CREAM, GENTLY WHIPPED TO SOFT PEAKS

For the stewed blueberries, place the blueberries, superfine sugar and rose geranium in a 8-cup capacity saucepan and place over medium heat. Gently cook for 14–18 minutes or until the blueberries start to break, then take off the stovetop, remove the rose geranium leaf and stalk and refrigerate until needed.

For the creamed rice pudding, place the rice and 4 cups of water in a 8-cup capacity saucepan and bring to a boil, then take off the heat and strain. Put the rice back into the pan and add the vanilla seeds and milk. Place the pan over medium heat and cook, stirring occasionally, for 15–20 minutes or until the rice is fully cooked or all the liquid has been absorbed. Take off the stovetop and stir in the sugar and gelatin until dissolved. Spread over a tray and refrigerate until set.

Once set, using a spatula, fold through the whipped cream, then pour into a serving dish and place back in the fridge to firm up. This should take 30 minutes.

To serve, take the rice pudding from the fridge, spoon over some of the stewed blueberries and the juices. Kapow! There you have it.

SPINACH, MUSTARD GREENS & BAKED RICOTTA CHEESE

This is the most simple and beautiful side to pork or beef, in fact, any main. I remember vividly the sublime taste and texture of a version of this I had for dinner at my friends' Jill and Andrew from Glenhora heritage farm. Their version was made with all sorts of goodies from their market garden. At Pope Joan, I have done many a version at times but mainly with nettles and Swiss chard. So with that in mind, you can change the garden leaves to almost anything you have growing. Try it with the tops of beets, broad (fava) bean and pea shoots.

⅔ CUP OLIVE OIL

1 BUNCH ENGLISH SPINACH, LEAVES PICKED, WASHED, SPUN DRY AND ROUGHLY CHOPPED

10 ½ OUNCES MUSTARD GREENS, WASHED, SPUN DRY AND ROUGHLY CHOPPED

2 SHALLOTS, THINLY SLICED

1 GARLIC CLOVE, THINLY SLICED

¼ TEASPOON FRESHLY GRATED NUTMEG

1 PINCH OF CAYENNE PEPPER

1 BIG PINCH OF FINE SEA SALT

¾ CUP FRESH RICOTTA CHEESE

2 FREE-RANGE OR ORGANIC EGG YOLKS

¾ CUP LIGHT CREAM

Preheat the oven to 450°F. Heat a 12 ¾ inch diameter skillet over high heat. Add the olive oil and, when hot, throw in the spinach, mustard greens, shallot and garlic and cook, stirring or tossing all the time, until wilted. Take off the heat and mix in the nutmeg, cayenne pepper and salt. Pour into a large bowl and, using a wooden spoon, fold in the ricotta.

Whisk the egg yolks and cream together in a small bowl. Pour into the ricotta mixture and mix well. Transfer to an ovenproof baking dish (measuring 8 inches in diameter) and bake for 20–25 minutes or until the ricotta has puffed up. Take out of the oven and serve immediately.

THE MRS' SWISS CHARD & FETA PIE

SERVES 4–6 (BUT WE MAKE IT FOR
TWO AND EAT THE REST THROUGH
THE WEEK FOR SNACKS AND LUNCH)

*When I met Sharlee, this was one of the first dishes she made for me and it's now a regular
at our dinner table. It's quite similar to spanakopita and the Swiss chard can easily
be changed to spinach if that's what you have growing.*

⅓ CUP OLIVE OIL

1 BUNCH SWISS CHARD, WASHED
AND ROUGHLY CHOPPED

½ TEASPOON FRESHLY GRATED NUTMEG

SEA SALT AND FRESHLY GROUND BLACK PEPPER

1 RED ONION, FINELY DICED

2 CUPS FETA CHEESE, CRUMBLED

1 TABLESPOON PINE NUTS

4 FREE-RANGE OR ORGANIC EGGS, BEATEN

5 ½ TABLESPOONS BUTTER, MELTED

10 SHEETS FILO PASTRY

2 TEASPOONS SESAME SEEDS

Preheat the oven to 350°F.

Heat a large skillet over medium heat, add the olive oil, Swiss chard and nutmeg, season with salt and pepper and cook for 2–3 minutes or until wilted. You may have to do this process in two batches. Remove from the heat and strain to drain the moisture.

Place the onion, feta and pine nuts in a large bowl and mix well. Add the Swiss chard and mix well to distribute the ingredients evenly. Add the beaten egg and stir to combine.

Take a pie dish (measuring about 9 ½ x 6 ½ x 2 ½ inches) and brush all over with the melted butter. Layer 2 sheets of filo lengthways in the pie dish and brush with the butter, then layer another 2 sheets of filo along the width and brush again with butter. Repeat this process so you have 4 double layers (and 2 sheets of filo remaining).

Spoon the Swiss chard mixture into the pie dish and spread evenly. Fold the overhanging filo over the filling to enclose, alternating between sides, brushing the top of the filo with butter. Place the last 2 sheets on top, tucking in the corners for a smooth finish, brush with butter and sprinkle with the sesame seeds. Using a fork, prick the top of the pie several times and bake for 50–60 minutes or until golden. Take out of the oven and leave to rest for 10 minutes before serving.

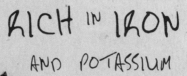

RICH IN IRON
AND POTASSIUM

ENGLISH RHYME

Tender-handed, stroke a nettle
And it stings you for your pains.
Grasp it like a man of mettle,
And it soft as silk remains.

ONE OF THE RICHEST SOURCES OF
CHLOROPHYLL IN THE VEGETABLE KINGDOM

CAN BE A TROUBLING WEED
AND MOWING CAN INCREASE
PLANT DENSITY

NETTLE

THE GROWTH OF STINGING NETTLE
IS AN INDICATOR THAT AN AREA HAS
HIGH FERTILITY AND HAS BEEN DISTURBED.

(URTICA DIOICA)

NETTLE

Who would have thought that this stinging little bugger would be so tasty?
I remember fondly watching Bedknobs and Broomsticks, *where I first*
encountered the idea of eating stinging nettles. I recall that as the children
turned up their noses at the thought of nettle soup, my nose did too.

THE ULTIMATE CURE-ALL

It wasn't until a good few years later when I had a most simple and tasty nettle soup with crab that I realized how good nettles really are. Like me, you may have the idea that they are (a) pretty vicious and (b) a weed, so what's the good in eating them? Well, history shows us that they have been used since the Bronze Age for a variety of purposes: as medicine, in weaving and eaten simply because they are nutrient rich. The ancient Greeks valued the nettle for its natural content of nutrients when eaten, but also as something of a cure-all. The list of complaints that were treated with the common garden-variety nettle and its uses is as long as it is varied: as a diuretic and laxative; to treat gangrene wounds, swellings, nose bleeds, pneumonia, asthma, tinea, bladder stones, worms, shingles, constipation, gout, sciatica, joint aches, dysentery, haemorrhoids, and bladder and kidney stones, not to mention fevers and eczema; as an antidote for poison and venomous stings; as a gargle for throat and mouth infections; and as an antiseptic for wounds and skin infections. So much relief from such an unassuming little plant, and one that is so often dismissed as a pest! The Greeks weren't the only ones to utilize the healing properties of the nettle. Native populations all over the globe have used the plant for centuries, from the ancient Romans to the native Americans.

Archaeologists have found nettle fiber used to make cloth, similar to flax or hemp.

Nettles are also exceptionally high in a naturally occurring chemical substance called chlorophyll, which is basically what makes plants green. This can be extracted from the plant and used as a dye for cloth and also foods.

FORAGING AND GROWING

So, where do you find them? Well, growing up in the UK they seemed to be everywhere, but on recent trips back there it seems they are most readily found along streams and embankments. In Australia, the most common place I have encountered them is, again, along streams and creeks, but you can also find them all over paddocks. They are said to be very good fodder for animals, with cattle and sheep producing more milk if nettles are introduced into their diet. (This would obviously have been a great advantage to farmers of ancient times.)

In terms of cultivating them in your backyard, it's usually unnecessary as, being a weed, they'll most likely infiltrate your garden on their own. So if you do find them, fight the urge to pull them out, and let them grow instead. They love soil that is rich in phosphates and nitrogen, so if they show themselves in your soil, you can take it as a good sign. They are hardy and will grow in full sun, but do very well in moist soil. Nettles also make a great liquid fertilizer. Soak the leaves in water for 1–2 weeks and spray the product on your garden. You will find this will also help to keep insects at bay. Also, make sure that you put any stems left over from your cooking into your compost. Compost loves nettles and will break down quicker when they're introduced.

HOW TO AVOID GETTING STUNG

So once they have grown and you want to pick them, how do you avoid getting stung? It helps to understand the plant a little bit. The sting is the nettle's own self-defence mechanism. If you look closely, you will see that the leaves are covered in what look like fine hairs. These hairs are very fragile and will break if touched, releasing chemicals that irritate the skin and cause a burning, stinging sensation.

The easiest way to avoid their sting is, thankfully, pretty much commonsense: when picking and handling nettles always wear a sturdy pair of gloves. Washing-up gloves are perfect as they are longer and will protect your wrists and forearms.

However, even the most seasoned nettle-forager will get stung every now and again, so here are some handy first-aid tips if you do. First of all is the dock plant, which is something of a companion to the nettle, in that they usually grow side by side. They have large leaves and a wide stem. Pluck the leaf and rub it on the affected area lightly. If you're not too confident at picking them out, then other cooling plants, such as a cucumber or parsley, will do just as well. Another remedy is to get a piece of sticky tape, place it over the sting, then pull it off to remove the sting. And, if all else fails, then you can spit on the area. It's surprizing the amount of natural healing properties in saliva. Gross but interesting. When you can, wash the area and pat dry. Don't rub!

COOKING

Once you have gathered your nettles, wash them really well. As with any plant that grows in soil, you want to wash it of dirt, but washing will also dislodge a majority of those pesky stinging hairs. All you need to do then to remove any remaining hairs is to plunge the nettles into a pot of boiling water and cook for 3–5 minutes, then drain and refresh in iced water. The iced water will halt the cooking process right away, and it also helps the plant retain its lovely bright green color. What you are left with are sting-free nettles that you can use much in the same way as you would spinach. Place the nettles in a tea towel and carefully wring out to extract as much excess water as you can, and store in the fridge or freezer until you want to use them.

NETTLE & CRAB RAVIOLI
WITH SWISS CHARD & GLASSWORT

SERVES 4

This is an adaption of a dish I did when I was head chef at Circa in Melbourne.
The subtle flavors marry beautifully together. The crab filling is kind of self-saucing
so make sure when wrapping the ravioli there are no air pockets or holes.

CRAB FILLING

7 OUNCES PICKED CRABMEAT
(I RECOMMEND SPANNER,
ALASKAN OR SNOW CRAB)

1 ¾ OUNCES CRÈME FRAÎCHE OR SOUR CREAM

JUICE OF ½ LEMON

FINE SEA SALT AND FRESHLY GROUND BLACK PEPPER

1 TEASPOON GOOD QUALITY GELATIN POWDER

1 FREE-RANGE OR ORGANIC EGG YOLK

2 TABLESPOONS FINE DRIED BREAD CRUMBS

1 TABLESPOON CHOPPED DILL

1 TABLESPOON CHOPPED
ITALIAN PARSLEY

NETTLE PASTA

1 LARGE BUNCH NETTLE, LEAVES PICKED

1 ¼ CUPS BREAD FLOUR

2 ¼ OUNCES FREE-RANGE OR ORGANIC
EGG YOLK (AT ROOM TEMPERATURE)

TO SERVE

1 ½ TABLESPOONS OLIVE OIL

1 SMALL BUNCH OF SWISS CHARD, THINLY
SLICED INCLUDING THE STEMS

1 CUP GLASSWORT (ALSO KNOWN AS SAMPHIRE)

3 ½ TABLESPOONS BUTTER, CHOPPED

4 TABLESPOONS PASTA COOKING WATER

EDIBLE FLOWERS, TO GARNISH

For the crab filling, place the crabmeat, crème fraîche, lemon juice and 1 tablespoon of water in a saucepan over low heat, season with salt and pepper and stir until everything is incorporated. Take it off the heat and mix in the rest of the ingredients until thoroughly combined. Transfer to a container and refrigerate for 1–1 ½ hours or until set.

For the nettle pasta, bring 6 cups of salted water to the boil. Add the nettles and cook for 5 minutes. Drain, refresh in icy cold water and wring out in a tea towel to remove as much moisture as possible. Place in a bowl and purée with a hand-held blender. (I recommend a hand-held blender rather than a normal standing blender as the amount to blitz is only a little and it's hard to purée finely in a bigger blender.) You should end up with 6 ⅓ ounces nettle purée but will need 2 ¼ ounces for this pasta, so freeze the rest for another use.

Note It's a good idea to weigh egg yolks when making pasta for accuracy, especially if you're using free-range or organic eggs, as they vary in size.

Place the nettle purée, flour, egg yolk and 1–2 tablespoons of water in the bowl of an electric mixer fitted with a dough hook attachment and mix on low speed for 3–4 minutes. The ingredients will not fully combine so place the dough onto a work surface and punch down for 5 minutes until combined and the dough is smooth. Leave to rest for 40 minutes or so, covered with a tea towel.

To make the ravioli, portion the nettle pasta dough into two. Roll each portion through a pasta machine, starting at the widest setting and moving down notch by notch until you have rolled it through setting number 2. One sheet will become the base of the ravioli and the other sheet will be the top. Take one sheet and cut it into 4 squares (about 4½ inches) and set aside—these will be your bases. Take the other sheet and roll through the pasta machine through setting number one, then cut into 4 squares, but a little bigger this time (about 5½ inches). Take the four base squares and lay on a lightly floured work surface. Divide the crab mixture into four, and place each portion in the center of a square, shaping the mixture into a small round. Now lightly brush the edges of the squares with a little water. Take a top square and lay it over the filling, gently squishing down around the filling so there are no air bubbles, then press the edges of the squares firmly to seal. Repeat for the remaining ravioli. Center a 3½ inch cutter around the filling and cut out the ravioli.

Bring 8 cups of salted water to the boil, add the ravioli and cook for 7 minutes.

While the ravioli are cooking, heat a large skillet over high heat, add the oil and Swiss chard and gently cook until wilted. Add the glasswort and butter and cook until the butter goes a nutty brown color, then add the pasta cooking water and cook until the sauce has emulsified. Spoon the Swiss chard mixture onto plates, drain the ravioli and place one on top of each. Garnish with the edible flowers to serve.

NETTLE & GREEN HERB SOUP WITH POACHED QUAIL EGG, SCALLOP & PANCETTA

SERVES 2

This soup is lovely on its own, but it does taste mighty fine with the added garnishes.
If poaching quail eggs sounds too finicky, then regular hen eggs will do just fine.

NETTLE & GREEN HERB SOUP

⅓ CUP WHITE WINE
(I RECOMMEND A SWEETER STYLE RIESLING)

⅓ CUP DRY VERMOUTH
(I LIKE TO USE NOILLY PRAT OR
YOU CAN JUST ADD MORE WINE)

2 GARLIC CLOVES, SLICED

1 LARGE SHALLOT, SLICED

1 EXTRA LARGE BUNCH OF ITALIAN PARSLEY,
LEAVES PICKED AND STALKS RESERVED

1 EXTRA LARGE BUNCH OF WATERCRESS,
LEAVES PICKED AND STALKS RESERVED

1 LARGE BUNCH NETTLES, LEAVES
PICKED AND WASHED

SEA SALT AND FRESHLY GROUND BLACK PEPPER

TO SERVE

3 TABLESPOONS WHITE VINEGAR

4 QUAIL EGGS (PLUS A FEW EXTRA
JUST IN CASE SOME BREAK)

1 ¾ OUNCES PANCETTA, CUT INTO LARDONS

4 LARGE SCALLOPS

SEA SALT AND FRESHLY GROUND BLACK PEPPER

JUICE OF ½ LEMON

For the nettle and green herb soup, first make a vegetable broth. Fill a 10-cup capacity saucepan with 4 cups of water and add the wine, vermouth, garlic, shallot and parsley and watercress stalks. Bring to a boil, then turn down the heat to medium and cook for about 40 minutes or until reduced to 2 cups. Take off the heat and strain the broth into a heatproof blender. Discard the solids (see Notes).

Wash the same pan and bring 6 cups of hot salted water to the boil. Cook the nettle and herbs for 7–8 minutes. Drain, add to the blender and blitz until a smooth purée (see Notes). Pass through a fine strainer, check the seasoning and if the soup is too thick, thin it out with a little water. Keep warm until ready to serve.

Meanwhile, prepare the garnishes to serve. Now, me giving you my method to poach quail eggs could make me look a little like a cowboy (an industry term for a "corner cutter" or cheat) to my peers but, hey, stuff 'em. My method makes the perfect poached quail eggs (but it doesn't work for regular hen eggs; see page 151 if you want to use hen eggs). Take two small dariole molds (also known as baba au rhum molds) and place half of the vinegar in each. Meanwhile, bring a saucepan half-filled with water to the boil, then turn down the heat to a simmer. Now carefully crack 2 quail eggs into each mold. I find it easier to crack through the shell if you use a serrated knife. Let the eggs stand in the vinegar for 30 seconds.

With a spoon, stir the water counter-clockwise, then tip in the eggs and vinegar and poach for 1–1 ½ minutes or until the whites are cooked but the yolks still oozy. Remove with a slotted spoon and pat dry on a tea towel.

Heat a small skillet over low heat and cook the pancetta until crispy (there's no need to add any oil). Drain off any fat and divide the pancetta between bowls.

Cut each scallop into four, season with salt and pepper and lemon juice and allow to marinate for 1 minute, then divide among the bowls. Place a poached quail egg in each bowl.

Place a bowl in front of your guests and serve the hot soup in a jug or soup terrine in the middle of the table for people to pour or ladle into the bowls themselves.

Notes The broth base for this soup is delicious and you can use it whenever vegetable broth is called for.

Be careful when blitzing hot mixtures in a blender. Always put a tea towel over the lid and, while holding down the lid, begin processing on low speed, working your way up. Many a time I have seen soup end up on the roof and on people's clothes. That aside, it can be dangerous and does hurt when hot liquids splash over your face.

NETTLE & SORREL SOUFFLÉ
OMELETTE WITH FETA

SERVES 2

There is nothing quite like waking up to an omelette for breakfast whether it be a normal rolled omelette or this one. It was on the Pope Joan menu for some time and is a must-try dish.

1 BUNCH NETTLES, LEAVES PICKED AND WASHED

6 FREE-RANGE OR ORGANIC EGGS

¾ CUP LIGHT CREAM

FINE SEA SALT AND FRESHLY GROUND BLACK PEPPER

1 SMALL BUNCH SORREL, THINLY SLICED

7 OUNCES FETA CHEESE
(I USE A SOFTER STYLE GOAT ONE)

Preheat the oven to 400°F.

Bring 4 cups of salted water to the boil. Add the nettles and cook for 5 minutes. Drain, refresh under cold water and wring out in a tea towel to remove as much moisture as possible, then roughly chop.

Whisk the eggs and cream together and season with salt and pepper. Stir in the nettle and the sorrel, reserving a little of the sorrel for garnish.

Divide the mixture between two baking dishes (each measuring about 6 ¼ diameter by 1 ¼ inches deep). Bake for 20 minutes, then remove from the oven immediately. Crumble over the feta cheese and scatter with the reserved sorrel. Serve straight away. A nice bit of toasted bread on the side is lovely with this.

Cultivated since the time of
ancient Egyptians where they
were seen as a symbol of
the universe

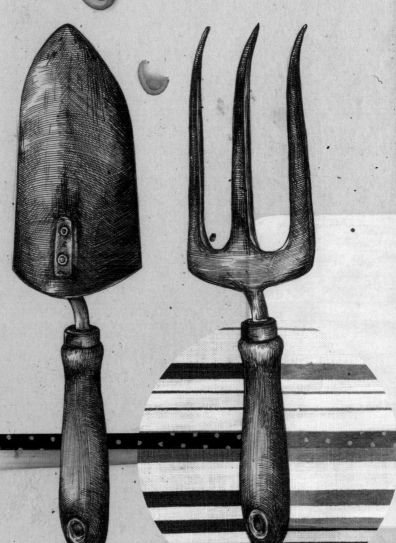

RELATED TO LILIES, GARLIC, LEEKS
SHALLOTS, CHIVES & ASPARAGUS

WERE AMONG EARLIEST RECORDS OF
VEGETABLES FOR SALE IN AUSTRALIA
AT THE PRICE of 2 SHILLINGS & 6 PENCE
PER OUNCE.

HARVEST
in 6-8 MONTHS

ONION

Eat them raw, sautéed, pickled, braised.
As the star of the dish or to complement,
their range of uses is so diverse.

(ALLIUM CEPA)

ONION

The vegetable that really epitomizes Barnsley and my youth is onion. Pickling onions, to be precise. Every year at the start of the season the Wilkinson men, Dad and Grandad Tom, would pickle a huge batch for the year. And, I have to say, that this year's batch we made at Pope Joan would have made them both proud.

COOKING

You may already know that there are many different types of onion. Here are just a few: shallot, scallion, salad onion, red (or Spanish) onion, white, brown, pickling … The list just goes on, and that's not even touching on the different variations of varieties, such as shallots and red salad onions.

Eat them raw, sautéed, pickled, baked, braised or in soup. As the star of the dish or to complement, their range of uses is so diverse. Of all the vegetables they are the only ones that go with all fishes, all meats and all seafood. Amazing.

They are also the universal vegetable, an integral base to just about every cuisine the world over. Their use extends back thousands of years—the ancient Egyptians worshipped them as a symbol of eternity, represented by their repetitive ring structure—and they have been praised and used both medicinally and culinarily by the Greeks, Romans and Indians since time immemorial.

However, you really need to put some thought into it and make sure you choose your onion variety wisely to complement what you are cooking it with. For example, shallot and scallions have very

delicate flavors. For sweetness, choose white. For something more robust, choose brown.

Personally, I tend to primarily use white onions. Even if I am just making a stew or soup, I will never use brown onions. Yes, they are cheaper but they have a different perfume and taste. To me brown onions impart a musty, earthy flavor, whereas, the white onion is the lady of the onion family. By comparison, she is perfumed, delicate, flavorsome and sweet.

TEARS ARE INEVITABLE

So why do they make you cry? Well, enough people have looked into why it happens and there are enough old wives' tales out there as to how to prevent it—soak them in water first, breathe through your mouth … My advice is: "Toughen up princess and just deal with it!" Peeling onions is always going to make you cry. If they're old and starting to ferment, they are going to make you cry. If they're young and fresh out of the ground, they're going to make you cry. Somewhere in the middle of the two they're not too bad, but just have a good cry, anyway.

PICKLING

I really should have included the Wilkinson pickling recipe, but if you really want to have a go at pickling them, just have a look through any old English or CWA cookbook and you'll find a recipe just as good. Here are some tips for you to get a great result:

- *The salting process is the most important part of the preparation. Onions need three days in salted water. Check daily that they remain submerged (weigh down with a plate if necessary). After three days, drain and wash them well.*

- *For the vinegar, most recipes ask for straight malt vinegar, but I like to mix in white or apple cider or some other variety to liven things up. Bring the vinegar to the boil, then pour over the onions.*

- *And last, but not least, the spices. You need mace, lots of black peppercorns, a little chili (dried is preferable), and one secret spice, which I really can't tell you or my father will kill me … Okay, okay, it's bay leaf.*

- *Pickle them for a good three or four months before eating—the longer the better really.*

GROWING AND STORAGE

If you want to try to grow your own onions and you haven't got a lot of space, try growing scallions from seed. You can plant them quite close together and they will do well in a pot or window box. If you want to try larger onions, red or white, I have found that the best results come from letting them shoot up and flower. When the flowers have gone, that is when the bulb underneath is ready to be harvested. Some people may say that is incorrect, but that is the way I've always grown them as I've found, if you take them out too early, the middle layers will still be green and will be immature in taste.

And as for storage, remember: they don't need to go in the fridge. Keep onions in a cool, dry place, like the bottom of your pantry. Also, leave the skins on until you're ready to use them.

BARNSLEY ONION SOUP

→ *MAKES 4 NICE BIG BOWLS OF SOUP*

I'm going to tell you a beautiful food story about my Mum's onion soup. She used to grow the onions herself in a small allotment near our house and the variety is one I have never heard of before or ever again. It seems it was an old heirloom variety that has just been kept in my family. The recipe I'm about to give you has been passed down for generations through my brood … Okay, that's a massive lie. For the record, Mum did make a great onion soup (and onion sauce to go with calf's liver and bacon), but this soup is just me playing around with the traditional French version—and having a go at the Frenchies at the same time. Stuff the French and their thinking that they invented the whole cuisine of the world. (Okay, okay, they did invent a lot and I do love them.) So I'm naming this soup after my hometown, made by a Barnsley fella in Australia with a French recipe.

⅔ CUP OLIVE OIL

3 ½ TABLESPOONS BUTTER

4 SMALL WHITE ONIONS, HALVED AND SLICED

4 SMALL RED ONIONS, HALVED AND SLICED

4 GARLIC CLOVES, SLICED

5 THICK-CUT SLICES SMOKED BACON, SLICED (OMIT IF VEGETARIAN)

½ CUP BRANDY

¼ CUP PORT

¾ CUP WHITE WINE

⅓ CUP RED WINE

¼ CUP ALL-PURPOSE FLOUR

8 CUPS HAM BROTH, VEGETABLE BROTH (SEE PAGE 187) OR JUST PLAIN OLD WATER

2 TABLESPOONS ITALIAN PARSLEY LEAVES, CHOPPED

SEA SALT AND FRESHLY GROUND BLACK PEPPER

Heat a saucepan (measuring 9 ½ inches in diameter by 6 ¼ inches deep) over medium–high heat and add the olive oil and butter. Once the butter has melted, add both types of onion, the garlic and bacon and cook for 20–25 minutes or until golden brown. Add the brandy and port, strike a match and carefully flame the alcohol. Once the flame has gone, add both the wines and cook until reduced by half.

Turn down the heat to low–medium and stir in the flour until there are no lumps. Add the broth, increase the heat and bring to a boil. Simmer for 50–60 minutes or until the soup is a thick broth consistency. To finish, add the parsley and season with salt and pepper to your liking. Serve with some bread.

A little tip This recipe also makes a lovely sauce for sausages, broiled liver and kidneys, chicken, pork and beef. All you have to do is reduce the liquid until a sauce consistency or that of thin gravy.

ROASTED SCALLIONS
WITH ROASTED PORK LOIN

SERVES 4 (WITH LEFTOVERS) OR 6

This is such a simple way to cook onions and can be done for any type , but I love the sweetness of cooked scallions with roasted pork. I would recommend the baked fennel, bread crumbs and herbs (see page 136) as a side. This is a good amount of pork to serve four with a generous amount left over for the next few days' lunch and dinner. Tell me, who doesn't love a cold roast pork sandwich?

ROASTED PORK LOIN

3 POUNDS 5 OUNCES PORK LOIN, SKIN FINELY SCORED

1 TABLESPOON SEA SALT

ROASTED SCALLIONS

1 TABLESPOON OLIVE OIL

6 LARGE SCALLIONS, CUT IN HALF (THERE'S NO NEED FOR PEELING)

3 TABLESPOONS SUPERFINE SUGAR

3 TABLESPOONS RED WINE VINEGAR

3 TABLESPOONS BUTTER

For the roasted pork loin, preheat the oven to 500°F.

Now, when buying your pork from the butcher, make sure he finely scores the skin for you. If you've got a piece that's not scored well, all you need is a new razor blade (the old school type) and carefully slice the pork skin at ½ inch intervals. Place in a roasting tray, scatter over the salt and massage it into the skin. Set aside for 10–15 minutes (and have that glass of wine we talked about).

Roast the pork for 1 hour, turning the tray 90 degrees every 15 minutes. After 1 hour, turn down the oven temperature to 325°F and continue roasting for 10–20 minutes.

Meanwhile, to make the roasted scallions, heat a large skillet over medium heat, add the olive oil, then the onion halves, cut side down, and cook for 2–3 minutes or until golden. Add the sugar and cook until a light caramel, shaking the pan occasionally. Add the vinegar and reduce to a glaze. Add the butter and ⅔ cup of water and stand back in case she spits. Turn down the heat and gently cook, adding a little more water if needed. After 15–20 minutes the onion should be soft. Turn the halves over and carefully remove from the pan. Take off the tough outer layers of the onions to serve.

Take the pork out of the oven and insert a metal skewer through the meat to test if it's ready; if the middle of the skewer is hot, then the pork is done. By this stage, you should now have the best crackling in town too. Place the pork on a plate and set aside to rest for 10–15 minutes, then slice and serve with the onions.

LIGHTLY PICKLED SHALLOTS

I don't know about you but for me a typical Sunday lunch when I was growing up consisted of some form of meat with its traditional side: chicken with sage stuffing, pork with apple sauce, lamb with mint sauce or beef with pickled sliced red onions. Now if I had been served this version of pickled onions back then, I would have jumped for joy—not that the onions served to me when I was young were bad ... It's only that these are a cracker, and can be used for all types of things. I like to add them to any type of leaf salad, mix them through any type of grain, serve them with poached or steamed fish, and they also make a great addition to a salad sandwich.

⅓ CUP RICE WINE VINEGAR

⅓ CUP APPLE CIDER VINEGAR

⅔ CUP SUPERFINE SUGAR

1 TEASPOON FINE SEA SALT

4 SHALLOTS, THINLY SLICED INTO RINGS AND SEPARATED

Place ⅔ cup of water, both the vinegars, the sugar and salt in a saucepan and bring to a boil, then take off the heat. Cool to room temperature and chill.

Place the shallot in a container and pour over the pickling liquid. They are best enjoyed fresh but they will keep for a few days in the fridge.

A little cheat's tip Add a nip of grenadine to the pickling liquid to dye the shallots an amazing pale pink color.

Name comes from the Latin word
'Pastus' meaing 'food'

CAN TAKE UP TO SIX MONTHS TO MATURE

Advisable to use fresh
seeds each year.

A few varieties are good all-rounders. One is
the Hollow Crown which is long and large and
the other is the Cobham, which is smaller but
has a lovely sweet flavor.

PARSNIP

RICH IN POTASSIUM &
DIETARY FIBER

PARSNIP

Parsnips are very similar to carrots to grow and use. They love the same style of soil, enjoy the same methods of cooking and, in fact, the word parsnip was once interchangeable with carrot in Europe. Combine this with the popularity of the white carrot variety at the time and you can see how it would have been easy to confuse the two. The main difference between them is that parsnip has a much earthier flavor and the texture is much more fibrous.

GROWING

Parsnips will grow all year round, but like carrot and beets, they can bolt to seed and become woody in summer. They do well in winter, but the cold will tend to slow their growth. They are really at their best in autumn and spring. Parsnips are not the easiest plant to grow first time around, especially from seed, but once you get a few crops you'll get the hang of it. The trick is, once planted, pat down the soil and keep the whole area really moist for three to four days after. Parsnips are frost tolerant, in fact, frost will improve their flavor, but they like to be kept moist. From seed to harvest should be four to five months.

VARIETIES

There are a few varieties I know of which are good all-rounders and relatively easy to grow, provided you have a nice sandy soil. One is the Hollow Crown, which is a quite long, large variety, and the other is the Cobham, which is relatively smaller but has a lovely sweet flavor. Parsnip varieties can be divided into three groupings based on shape. These are bulbous (or round), bayonet and wedge. The bayonet is fairly straight up and down. The wedge is the type that most of us will recognize, with its broad shoulders and tapered waist. They can vary slightly in color but really only from a creamy white color to a yellow-white. The main difference will be length, width, and, of course, flavor. So try a few different ones and decide for yourself which type you prefer.

THROUGH THE AGES

The modern parsnip that we recognize today is the offspring of the wild parsnip, which can still be found growing on roadsides and in fields all over Europe. It's pretty thin and spindly looking. Not much chop really when compared to the lovely fat parsnips of today. It is thought that the Romans were the first to properly cultivate the parsnip. It is a member of the *Umbelliferae* (also called *Apiaceae*) family, which is a group of hollow-stemmed, aromatic plants that include the likes of parsley, chervil and of course, my favorites, carrots.

The parsnip waned in popularity in France, where instead they fed it to their pigs. Parsnip-fed pig was thought to be a very fine delicacy. This practice is still used in Italy to raise pigs for prosciutto. Parsnip is also used as a flavoring in some Irish beers.

COOKING

When cooking them, I find you will have a better result if you steam parsnips rather than boil them because of their naturally high starch content. They can go quite gluggy if boiled, which is not very desirable. Also, because of their high sugar content, parsnips roast extremely well. Just peel the outside skin and cut into quarters lengthways. I always remove the core, as it is very astringent and quite indigestible (apart from those in very young parsnips). Then just toss them in a bit of oil and seasoning and roast. Delicious. Or try roasted parsnips with a honey glaze—it is an absolute classic and one of my favorite vegetable side dishes. I didn't include a recipe for it, as I figured everyone is probably already familiar with it or have their mom's recipe, but if you're not or you don't, don't worry. It is very easy to make. Just put your parsnips in a flameproof roasting tray on the stovetop and cook until you get a nice bit of color on them. Then deglaze the pan with some honey and a little bit of nice vinegar, like a white wine or chardonnay. Put the pan straight into a hot oven and roast until lovely and tender. That's it. Then into a bowl and onto the table. Yum!

PARSNIP & BLACK RICE RISOTTO WITH OR WITHOUT LOBSTER

SERVES 6

Parsnip adds a wonderful rich, earthy flavor, especially when combined with sweet mascarpone and seafood. Although I have written this "with or without lobster" give it a try "with" for me. Parsnip is often overlooked as an accompaniment for seafood, but it binds really well, adding a real richness.

PARSNIP, MASCARPONE & HORSERADISH PURÉE

5 LARGE PARSNIPS

3 ½ TABLESPOONS BUTTER

3 TABLESPOONS OLIVE OIL

⅔ CUP MASCARPONE

3 ½ OUNCES HORSERADISH PURÉE (FROM A JAR)

RISOTTO

⅓ CUP OLIVE OIL

2 CUPS BLACK ARBORIO RICE (SEE NOTE)

⅓ CUP WHITE WINE

8 OUNCES COOKED LOBSTER MEAT

1 CUP CHOPPED DILL AND CHERVIL

JUICE OF 2 LEMONS

SEA SALT AND FRESHLY GROUND BLACK PEPPER

For the purée, top, tail, peel and core the parsnips, keeping all the scraps. Place the scraps and 6 cups of water in a saucepan and bring to a boil, then simmer for 15 minutes. Set the broth aside and return to a simmer when ready to make the risotto. (This is an excellent broth for all vegetarian dishes.)

Meanwhile, thinly slice the peeled parsnips. Heat a large skillet, add the butter and olive oil over low heat, add the parsnip and sweat for 2–3 minutes. Turn up the heat, add 1 ¼ cups of water, bring to a boil and cook for 7–9 minutes or until the parsnip is tender. Strain, reserving the cooking juices. Blitz the cooked parsnip in a food processor with the mascarpone and horseradish purée until smooth. If necessary, add a little of the reserved juices to thin out the blitzed purée to the consistency of mashed potato.

For the risotto, heat a large heavy-bottomed skillet heat over medium heat, add the olive oil and heat for 1 minute. Add the rice, stir to coat and cook for 2–3 minutes or until coated. Add the wine and cook out for 3–5 minutes or until evaporated. Gradually add the hot broth, 1 cup at a time, stirring frequently, allowing each addition to be absorbed before adding the next, until the rice has absorbed all the broth and is cooked. Take off the heat, fold in the parsnip purée, then return to the heat. To finish, stir through the lobster, herbs and lemon juice and season with salt and pepper.

Note Why black Arborio rice? For me, the nuttier flavor of the black rice gives the parsnip an extra kick. If you can't find black Arborio rice, regular white Arborio rice is fine but it will not need as much cooking.

PARSNIP CHIPPIES

MAKES ROUGHLY THE SAME AMOUNT
AS FOUND IN A GOOD-SIZED BAG OF
POTATO CHIPS

This is such a delicious snack that it makes its bought potato counterpart look like one of Cinderella's stepsisters. These beauties are an awesome quick snack, great with a beer watching football, as a canapé or even as an alternative to potato chips for the kids' dinners. They're fun to make with the kids too. Don't be scared to fry in the home. Yes, you need a deep-fryer and yes, of course, they are fried, but they taste delicious. As long as you have a thermometer and your oil doesn't heat to above 400°F, you should be fine. Obviously, you need to observe this task very closely. Try making chips from other root vegetables such as carrot, sweet potato and even lotus root, but my favorite is the parsnip. The chippies will stay crispy for about 6 hours if you would like to pre-fry them as a snack before a dinner party.

4 CUPS VEGETABLE OR SUNFLOWER
OIL, FOR DEEP-FRYING

1 REGULAR OR 2 SMALL PARSNIPS
(ABOUT 10½ OUNCES IN TOTAL)

SEA SALT OR HERB SALT (SEE PAGE 279)

Heat the oil in a deep-fryer to 315°F or in a deep saucepan (no more than one-third full). Peel the parsnip and top and tail, then make wafer-thin slices either on a mandoline or simply peel into slices using long strokes.

Place a frying basket into the hot oil, add a handful of parsnip slices and cook for 30 seconds, then lift the basket. Leave for 1–2 minutes, then submerge again in the oil and fry until golden brown. This blanching step helps crispen up the parsnip. Tip the chips out onto a tray lined with paper towels to absorb the excess oil, and repeat with the remaining parsnip slices. Pour the drained chips into a bowl, sprinkle with the salt and enjoy with a nice cold beer.

PARSNIP SKORDALIA

MAKES 2 CUPS

Such a simple yet pleasant recipe, this is my twist on the classic skordalia, usually made with potatoes. I love the sweet earthy flavor that the parsnip adds, not to mention the texture of the hazelnuts and garlic flavor rounding everything out at the end. It's essential to remove the woody core of the parsnip or your purée will be stringy and I prefer to use skim milk as it helps prevent scorching.

¼ CUP HAZELNUTS (SEE NOTE)	JUICE OF ½ LEMON
3½ OUNCES ORGANIC GARLIC CLOVES, BLANCHED TWICE IN SALTED BOILING WATER	3 TABLESPOONS EXTRA VIRGIN OLIVE OIL
1 LARGE PARSNIP, PEELED, CORED AND THINLY SLICED (SEE NOTE)	1 TABLESPOON FINELY CHOPPED ITALIAN PARSLEY
1 ⅔ CUPS SKIM MILK	SEA SALT AND FRESHLY GROUND BLACK PEPPER

Preheat the oven to 350°F. Place the hazelnuts on a baking sheet and roast for 5–10 minutes. Place in a tea towel and rub off the skins while still warm.

Place the garlic, parsnip, hazelnuts and milk in a saucepan, bring to a boil, then reduce to a simmer and cook until the parsnip is tender. Pass through a fine strainer, reserving both the solids and cooking liquid. Pulse the parsnip mixture in a blender or use a hand-held stick blender until a chunky purée, adding a little of the reserved cooking liquid to achieve the consistency of a purée. Stir through the lemon juice, olive oil and parsley and season with salt and pepper to finish.

Note If you want to make a more traditional skordalia, replace the parsnip with potato and the roasted hazelnuts with blanched almonds (not roasted).

THERE ARE ABOUT

4000

POTATO VARIETIES
WORLDWIDE

SOIL pH
of 5.5 – 6

First domesticated in Peru
between 8000bc & 5000bc

AUSTRALIA'S LARGEST VEGETABLE CROP. ACCOUNTING FOR WELL OVER A THIRD OF VEGETABLE PRODUCTION. WORLD'S FOURTH LARGEST FOOD CROP

POTATO

There is nothing quite like digging your own potatoes from the ground, washing them and serving them simply.

POTATO

Where to start, with a vegetable like the perfect potato? The potato is to the Western world what rice is to the East. An irreplaceable staple, loved, respected and revered.

PERFECT MASH EVERY TIME

My first experience in the world of cooking and learning how to construct a dish was being told to think of the protein component, think about which way to cook the potato to go with it, and then think about what other vegetables to include. There was no question of not using potato. When I was first learning to cook we just used potatoes with everything. Even now, when there are so many different starches I like to use (rice or grains, for instance), it is still one of my favorite things. Who doesn't love thinly sliced potatoes, cooked through with cream, thyme and garlic, pressed into a dauphinoise? It's a classic.

But then, there is nothing finer than perfect mashed potato. And I'm not talking instant mash, but a proper mash, creamy and perfectly seasoned. The secret is in the ratio: 50 per cent potato to 50 per cent butter, with a bit of milk to bind it. It's not diet food, obviously but, if you are going to indulge every once in a while, then do it properly. Thin it out with a bit of milk and season with salt, but no pepper. It's the best mash ever, I promise you— give it a go. And trust me on the no-pepper thing.

USES

The potato arrived in Europe from the Andean region of South America, thanks to the Spanish conquerors around the late 1500s, who referred to them as "patatas." Though they were originally viewed with great suspicion (as something on the verge of being outright poisonous), by the 1700s they had begun to be accepted, grown in many countries and widely used.

So it has only been around for about 400 years. That's all the time that we have had them. It's almost unbelievable because, like the tomato, they have become so invaluable to us in that period. During that time, potatoes have become essential to the lives of entire populations. In Prussia, after the great famine of 1774, Frederick the Great recognized the potato's potential to save his people from starvation, and so ordered them to be sent to the populace for free.

In Ireland, the potato was recognized very early for its high yield for very little labor—an acre ($^2/_5$ hectare) of potatoes was enough to feed a family of six for a year. The Irish tenant farmers were, at the time, some of the poorest people in the Western world, and this vegetable was seen as a godsend, allowing them to work their land and provide sustenance for their families. That is until 1845 when disease, potato blight, caused the year's crop to fail and the subsequent deaths of more than one million Irish due to starvation over the next six years. As a result, one million Irish migrated to the Americas, leaving Ireland a shell of its former self. All those jokes about the Irish and their love and dependency on the potato. When you put it into context, it isn't really a laughing matter.

GROWING

When I was a kid, we always grew potatoes. Dad always had them in the garden. And we were lucky because in the UK, we experienced three seasons every year compared to areas like Scandinavia or Russia, where it's so cold they only enjoy one. Perhaps that's why I thought it would be a good idea to get a job in my early teens on a big potato farm just outside of Penistone, near Barnsley.

I lasted one day. I was getting paid around one-and-a-half pounds an hour to dig potatoes, and I am not exaggerating when I say it was the hardest, most rubbish job in the world.

Still, we're not talking commercial scale if you want to grow a few in the backyard. And there is nothing quite like digging your own potatoes from the ground, washing them and serving them simply—boiled and smashed with a bit of good olive oil, chardonnay vinegar, salt and fresh herbs. Perfect.

One thing I will recommend is to put them in only one area of your garden only. Go to a nursery or garden center and invest in a potato sack or bed exclusively for potatoes because once they are in they will simply keep growing. For example, at my new house I put a new garden bed in and I virtually sifted the soil to make sure it was nice and clean to start. But I must have missed one or two little potatoes (probably no bigger than the size of my pinky fingernail) and, within the space of a few months, I had potatoes everywhere again. Once they're in, they're in. I saw a great technique on an old farm in Derbyshire, UK,

where the farmer had collected old truck tyres, filled them full of soil and used those to contain the potatoes and stop them spreading throughout the entire garden.

VARIETIES

One thing that may hold people back is what variety to plant or use. There are so many, literally thousands of, potato varieties worldwide, and around 500 available for a home gardener to grow. So when you are choosing potatoes, look for the best type for what you want to do. If you are at the supermarket or grocer, talk to the produce people. If you're at a farmers' market, take the chance to talk to a farmer. It really makes such a difference to your dish to pick the right one for the right purpose. It's comparable in cooking terms with apples, with the French referring to the potato as the "pomme de terre" (the apple of the earth) because, like the apple, potatoes have different varieties that are better suited to different cooking methods. As with apples, you have baking, cooking and eating ones, and it's the same with the potato. Some are good "all rounders," like the Desiree, Coliban or Royal Blue. Some are better for mashing, like the King Edward. For boiling, try the Pink Fir Apple, Fingerling or Nicola varieties, especially if you're wanting to make a salad. The Toolangi Delight is a variety that is excellent to bake for a nice light gnocchi. If you're wanting to fry a good homemade chip, variety is all important, because the outcome depends on the level of starch within a particular variety. And I have found that the Russet Burbank, Golden Wonder and Yukon Gold are the kings of frying potatoes. Unfortunately, for the general populace, the big fast-food chains know this as well and secure around 90 per cent of the crop for their fries. No wonder we love them so much!

THE BEST SIMPLE LITTLE ROAST SPUDS

SERVES 4

Look out for small cocktail potatoes, weighing about 1 ½ ounces each, to make this simple recipe.
I'd recommend either fingerlings or marble-sized new potatoes.

20 SMALL POTATOES

SEA SALT, OR HERB SALT (SEE PAGE 279)

½ CUP FATBACK (OR OLIVE OIL IS
THE HEALTHIER OPTION)

Preheat the oven to 500°F.

Wash the potatoes with a sponge, but don't scrub them too hard as you really want to keep the skin, then dry them off with a tea towel. Place in a saucepan, making sure you have at least 2 inches from the top, and fill with enough cold water to just cover the potatoes. Bring to a boil over high heat, then continue to cook for 5 minutes. Drain and let the steam evaporate.

Meanwhile, place the fat in a deep-sided heavy-bottomed roasting tray and heat in the oven for 2–4 minutes. Take the tray out, add the potatoes and place back into the oven. Turn down the oven temperature to 425°F and continue baking for 35–50 minutes, shaking the tray every 8 minutes or so. Take out of the oven and drain off the excess fat. Sprinkle with salt or herb salt if you have some handy.

BRAISE OF FINGERLING POTATOES
WITH SEA BASS

SERVES 4

*This recipe is so adaptable, for many reasons. It is so delicious and, although it is quite rich,
it is one of my favorite dishes to eat in any weather or season. For the spuds, you can use any good waxy
small potato that likes to be braised. You can also take out the sea bass and tomatoes or replace
it with another fish, but it has to be a meaty one—you know the types: ones that will not dry
out easily when braised, such as cod. Now you're asking what this goes with? Well, I'm not going
to tell you but here's a clue—have a look through the rest of the book and decide what recipe
it may marry well with. Or eat simply with some couscous or even a little polenta.*

¾ CUP EXTRA VIRGIN OLIVE OIL

2 LARGE WHITE ONIONS, HALVED
AND THINLY SLICED

6 SMALL FINGERLING POTATOES,
WASHED AND SLICED TO THE THICKNESS
OF A BEER-BOTTLE TOP

2 TOMATOES, PREFERABLY HEIRLOOMS OF ANY
VARIETY, OTHERWISE PLUMS, ROUGHLY CHOPPED

SEA SALT AND FRESHLY GROUND BLACK PEPPER

1 POUND 5 OUNCES SEA BASS (ASK YOUR
FISHMONGER TO REMOVE ALL SKIN AND BONE),
CUT INTO 7 x 2 ¾ INCH PORTIONS (SEE NOTE)

3 TABLESPOONS SALTED BABY CAPERS, RINSED

JUICE OF 1 LEMON

½ BUNCH ITALIAN PARSLEY, LEAVES
PICKED AND ROUGHLY CHOPPED

Heat a heavy-bottomed saucepan (measuring 10½ inches in diameter by 6¼ inches deep) over medium
heat. Add the olive oil and heat for 3 minutes, then add the onion and cook, stirring occasionally, for 8
minutes or until they start to break down but have not started to color. Add the potato and cook, stirring
occasionally, for 10 minutes. Add the tomato and cook, stirring occasionally, for 5 minutes or until it starts
to break down. At this point, season with salt and pepper, increase the heat to high, add 2 ⅔ cups of
council pop (as my grandfather use to say, that is water) and bring to a boil. Turn down to low heat and cook
out for 15–20 minutes or until the potatoes are cooked.

Now add the sea bass, turn up the heat to high and cook for 4 minutes. Take the pan immediately off the
heat, stir in the capers, cover with a lid and set aside for 10–15 minutes.

Take the lid off and have a look to see if the fish is cooked. If it's ready, check the seasoning and put back over
medium to gently heat. Add the lemon juice and parsley and serve.

Note If you can't get sea bass, give cod or maco shark a try.

"SHEPHERD'S PIE" CROQUETTES

MAKES 30–50 (DEPENDING
ON YOUR PREFERRED SIZE)

Okay, so it ain't literally a shepherd's pie but all the ingredients are what you would put into one. Cooking lamb shoulder slowly in a slow cooker is a great way to make the most of this cut. The croquettes make a lovely canapé, snack or side for a main of lamb, of course. However, they are a little time consuming so don't try them when you get home from work—give 'em a go on your day off instead.

1 POUND 12 OUNCES BONELESS LAMB FOREQUARTER SHOULDER

1 CARROT, PEELED AND DICED

1 SMALL TURNIP, PEELED AND DICED

1 WHITE ONION, QUARTERED

2 POUNDS 4 OUNCES MASHED POTATO (WITH NOTHING ADDED BUT MAKE SURE IT IS STILL WARM)

2 TABLESPOONS DIJON MUSTARD

4 TABLESPOONS MELTED DUCK FAT, COOLED TO ROOM TEMPERATURE (OR OLIVE OIL)

1 CUP CHOPPED ITALIAN PARSLEY

SEA SALT AND FRESHLY GROUND BLACK PEPPER

3 TABLESPOONS SHERRY VINEGAR

CRUMB

⅔ CUP ALL-PURPOSE FLOUR

8 FREE-RANGE OR ORGANIC EGGS, LIGHTLY BEATEN

10 CUPS FRESH BREAD CRUMBS (MADE FROM 2 LOAVES OF CRUSTLESS WHITE BREAD)

VEGETABLE OIL, FOR DEEP-FRYING

Place the lamb shoulder, carrot, turnip and onion in a slow cooker and cover with water. Cook on high for 7 hours. Once cooked, cool slightly, then take out the meat and shred into a bowl. Pass through a strainer, discarding the cooking liquid. Add the vegetables to the bowl. Mix in the remaining ingredients, then shape about ¼ cup of the mixture into croquettes. This will make 30 or you could make them a bit smaller to yield 50.

To crumb, place the flour, eggs and 1 ⅔ cups of the bread crumbs in separate bowls. Dip a croquette into the flour, then into the egg, then the bread crumbs and place on a tray. Repeat with the remaining croquettes, topping up the bread crumbs as needed as they get a bit messy from the egg. After you have crumbed all the croquettes, repeat dipping in the egg and bread crumbs again so they are double crumbed.

Heat the oil in a deep-fryer to 350°F or in a deep saucepan (no more than one-third full) and deep-fry the croquettes, in batches, for 2–3 minutes or until golden and hot on the inside. Sprinkle with salt (or herb salt, see page 279) and serve straight away.

WINTER SALAD OF FINGERLING & PURPLE CONGO POTATOES, CAPOCOLLO & TRUFFLE

SERVES 4 AS AN ENTRÉE OR A SALAD OR SIDE TO SHARE

I have to admit, if you do have a spare truffle hanging around, this dish bloody rocks with it shaved over … But if you don't, it's lovely just as is. This salad must be served warm to get the best flavor out of the potatoes.

6 SMALL FINGERLING POTATOES, WASHED AND CUT INTO ½ INCH THICK SLICES	2 TABLESPOONS SALTED BABY CAPERS, RINSED AND CHOPPED
6 SMALL PURPLE CONGO POTATOES, WASHED AND CUT INTO ½ INCH THICK SLICES	1 BUNCH PARSLEY SHOOTS, TRIMMED (OR FINELY CHOPPED ITALIAN PARSLEY)
1 QUANTITY TARRAGON EMULSION (SEE PAGE 277)	⅓ CUP EXTRA VIRGIN OLIVE OIL
1 QUANTITY PARSNIP SKORDALIA (SEE PAGE 210)	SEA SALT AND FRESHLY GROUND BLACK PEPPER
8 THIN SLICES CAPOCOLLO (USE PROSCIUTTO OR SALAMI IF YOU CAN'T FIND IT)	1 SMALL WINTER TRUFFLE

Place the two types of potatoes each in a large saucepan, add enough cold water to just cover and add some salt. Bring to a boil, then turn down the heat to a simmer and cook for 5–7 minutes or until just cooked. Insert the tip of a sharp knife into the potato slices to check if they're ready; if the knife goes in easily, they're cooked. Drain straight away and place in a bowl. Toss with some of the tarragon emulsion so they are really well coated and leave to sit for 1 minute. Spread or spoon some of the skordalia over the base of a large serving plate, spoon the potato on top, scatter over the capocollo, capers and parsley shoots, drizzle with the olive oil, season with salt and pepper and finely shave the truffle over the top to finish.

Note Capocollo is cured, air-dried rolled pork. It's available from good Italian delicatessens.

POTATO SCALLOPS

MAKES 20

We've all seen them before, usually in a hot-food display cabinet at a takeaway food shop. I have to own up that my school-dinner money went to buying potato scallops from the local fish shop. I love them. This recipe is adapted from a small element of a dish that I used to make at Vue de Monde. Okay, so it's junk food, but million-dollar junk food done this way. And, if you're flush, buy a winter truffle, thinly slice it and put a slice on each side of the scallop before battering and deep-frying.

3 LARGE ALL-PURPOSE POTATOES

3 ¼ CUPS LIGHT CREAM

2 PINCHES OF FINE SEA SALT

30 TURNS OF WHITE PEPPER FROM A MILL

VEGETABLE OIL, FOR DEEP-FRYING

HERB SALT (SEE PAGE 279), TO SERVE

BATTER

1⅓ CUPS ALL-PURPOSE FLOUR

1 ½ CUPS CORNSTARCH

3 TABLESPOONS BAKING POWDER

FINE SEA SALT

ABOUT 2 CUPS SPARKLING MINERAL WATER

Preheat the oven to 450°F. Line the base and sides of a baking sheet (measuring 10½ x 8 x 2½ inches) with parchment paper. Give the potatoes a quick wash, leave the skin on, top and tail them, then slice into ½ inch thick slices. You should get roughly 20 slices. Place the cream in a 8-cup capacity saucepan and bring to a boil, stirring occasionally. Take off the heat and season with salt and pepper. Pour into the baking sheet, arrange the potato slices in the tray, cover with foil, pierce the foil with 5 holes and bake for 30 minutes. Insert a skewer through the sliced potato to test if it is cooked—it should give a bit of resistance. Take out of the oven and leave to cool.

1 *Slice the potatoes.*

2 *Pour the cream into a lined baking sheet.*

3 *Place the potato slices in the cream. Cover with foil and bake in the oven.*

Meanwhile, make the batter. Mix the dry ingredients together in a bowl and make a well in the center. Slowly add enough of the mineral water and whisk in until you have a thick smooth batter (see Note).

Once the potatoes have cooled, carefully take the slices out of the cream and layer onto a tray. (Strain the cream and use to make mashed potato.)

Heat the vegetable oil in a deep-fryer to 315°F or in a deep saucepan (no more than one-third full). Carefully dip each potato slice in the batter and deep-fry, in batches, for 2–3 minutes or until golden. Sprinkle with the herb salt and serve straight away.

Note This is my standard batter, which I use for most things. It's a great recipe to add to your repertoire. For this version, the batter needs to be thick so that it sticks to the potato. If you want to use the batter for other recipes, frying fish or vegetables say, then add a splash more mineral water so it's not as thick.

4 Once the potatoes are cooked and have cooled, carefully take the slices out of the cream and layer onto a tray.

5 Prepare the oil for frying. Dip each potato slice in batter.

6 Fry scallops in batches until golden.

Diverse group of frost-tender annuals and perennials has varied shapes, sizes, colors and patterns. Individual fruits can weigh from 2 lbs to 1300 lbs.

PUMPKINS
LOVE SPACE

Look at the love affair Americans have with pumpkin. Americans have made this veg famous with Halloween jack-o-lanterns and the all-American pumpkin pie.

TAKE BETWEEN 70-120 DAYS TO MATURE

PUMPKIN AND SQUASH

OLDEST EVIDENCE OF PUMPKIN SEEDS ARE FOUN IN MEXICO DATING BETWEEN 7000 & 5000BC

PUMPKIN AND SQUASH

For pumpkin and squash to be included in here, among my all-time favorite vegetables is, to be completely honest with you, a bit of a revelation. I have nothing against pumpkin and squash itself, but culturally, to myself and many other Englishmen, they were always seen primarily as pigs' fodder. And I'll confess it took me a while to come to terms with eating them as a staple vegetable side. But once I was on the pumpkin and squash trail, I must admit to being jealous of those English pigs!

PUMPKIN AND SQUASH EATERS

It is strange to consider that the countries where pumpkin has been most heartily embraced are where I guess the options were limited. In Australia and America, the early settlers would have needed to have accepted and used the plants which would yield the highest return for their investment of labor because realistically the climates were tough and unlike anything they had seen before and the landscape would have seemed terribly barren and unfriendly. They had to embrace the things that would shield their families from the threat of starvation. It seems so remote now to us, with our supermarkets open all hours and food never far away, but this was a genuine concern to our forebears.

It is thought that pumpkin originated in America, and they have certainly made them famous with Halloween jack-o'-lanterns and the all-American pumpkin pie. In England we hollowed out turnips for All Hallow's Eve for some reason. And I know for a fact that I had never even considered there was such a thing as a pumpkin scone before I arrived in Australia!

COOKING

There is a natural sweetness within pumpkin that at times has notes of different spices like cloves or licorice. I like to add some licorice to my pumpkin purée to really enhance the aniseed flavor that is already there. The great thing about it is, like potato, it can be cooked just about every way: steamed, roasted, thinly sliced or broiled. Just don't boil it, please. It loses all its integrity and turns into a horrid nondescript orange mush.

A lot of people forget that you can also use the seeds. Just wash and then dry them out in the oven or even in the sun. Toss these through a salad, either toasted or raw, for an interesting textural element. They also make a great garnish for cakes, like one of my favorites the hummingbird, with its lemony cream cheese frosting and lightly toasted shredded coconut. Alternatively, combine them with some of your favorite nuts and dried fruits as a homemade trail-mix snack. So versatile. And that's just the seeds.

And surely if you have a child, pumpkin purée is a must. It has good vitamin A and C content, and is low in salt and saturated fat, making it a tasty, healthy option for young 'uns. It also contains considerable iron, making it a good choice for vegetarians.

Pumpkin obviously works well as a side with any roast meat—it's one of my favorites—but it is also an incredible match with seafood and salty meats, like salami or duck leg confit; the salt of the meat and the sweetness of the pumpkin enhance each other's flavor wonderfully.

VARIETIES

There really is a lot to love about pumpkin as a gardener. There are lots of different varieties to choose from, depending on your taste. If you prefer your pumpkin large, then select the Queensland blue (a.k.a. ironbark) or Japanese varieties, whereas if you like them small try the kent or the gem, which grow to about the size of an onion. My favorite is the butternut squash, which is nutty, sweet, a great all-rounder and the best choice for cakes or biscuits. The skin is so thin you can leave it on when roasting to add flavor and texture.

GROWING

One word of warning when considering growing pumpkin: when you've selected your variety and bought the seedlings at the nursery, now, unless you have acres of space, just plant one of the seedlings (often they come in threes). Trust me. Once the seedling has established, it grows like a weed! And if you let it, it will not only take up a lot of room but it will also climb pretty much everywhere. You can train it and point it in a certain direction and, if you like, it will grow up a tree or up a fence. Remember to keep cutting the vines back, though, or your neighbors will end up with all your pumpkin! For all the space that the plant does require, they really don't produce that much fruit, but they are so tasty, it's definitely worth it.

And, once the season is over for the year, make sure you save yourself some seeds from the fruit. You can dry them out in the sun, then put them in an envelope, and don't forget to write down which variety they are for replanting next year.

Pumpkin can also assist in keeping a healthy garden. Save the waste or skin to use in your compost as it breaks down very quickly.

ROASTED BUTTERNUT SQUASH & HEIRLOOM CARROT, MACADAMIAS, CAPER & RAISIN DRESSING

*SERVES 2 AS AN ENTRÉE SALAD
OR 4 AS A SIDE*

½ BUNCH HEIRLOOM CARROTS

1 BUTTERNUT SQUASH, PEELED, SEEDS REMOVED AND DICED

OLIVE OIL, FOR COATING

1 TABLESPOON HONEY

3 TABLESPOONS ROASTED MACADAMIA NUTS, CHOPPED

3 TABLESPOONS CHOPPED MINT

3 TABLESPOONS CHOPPED ITALIAN PARSLEY

7 OUNCES SOFT FETA CHEESE

CAPER & RAISIN DRESSING

1 TABLESPOON SALTED BABY CAPERS, RINSED

1 TABLESPOON RAISINS, SOAKED FOR 5 MINUTES IN WARM WATER, THEN DRAINED

3 ANCHOVY FILLETS

1 RED BIRD'S EYE CHILI, HALVED, SEEDS REMOVED AND CHOPPED

1 GARLIC CLOVE, CRUSHED

5 BASIL LEAVES

2 TEASPOONS BALSAMIC VINEGAR

JUICE OF ½ LEMON

⅓ CUP EXTRA VIRGIN OLIVE OIL

SEA SALT AND FRESHLY GROUND BLACK PEPPER

For the caper and raisin dressing, add all the solid ingredients to a large mortar and pound to a sticky paste consistency. Add all the liquid ingredients and taste for seasoning. Add salt and pepper if needed but remember the anchovies and capers are naturally salty. Set aside.

Preheat the oven to 375°F. Peel the carrots, place in a saucepan of cold salted water and bring to a boil, then drain. Place the squash in a large roasting tray and generously coat with the olive oil. Roast for 10 minutes, turning once, then throw in the semi-cooked carrots and roast for a further 10 minutes or until they are both cooked. Brush with the honey and place in a bowl to cool.

Once at room temperature, dress the vegetables with some of the caper and raisin dressing and toss with some of the macadamias and some of the herbs. Place neatly into desired bowl, then garnish with the remaining macadamias and herbs, a little more of the dressing and crumble over the feta cheese.

BUTTERNUT SQUASH MASH WITH FISH FINGERS

SERVES 4–6 (PLUS SPARE
FISH FINGERS FOR THE FREEZER)

Okay, okay, you got me on this recipe. It's actually all about the fish fingers ... but who doesn't love a fish finger? The butternut squash mash part is easy and could go with anything. The fish fingers are a little tricky but the recipe makes plenty so freeze them for a later date or, for a less time-consuming preparation (but just as enjoyable), you can make the fish mixture into cakes.

FISH FINGERS

3 LARGE GOOD-MASHING POTATOES, PEELED AND DICED INTO CHUNKS

6 CUPS MILK

3 POUNDS 5 OUNCES WHITE FISH TRIM (BONELESS OFF-CUTS, I'D ASK YOUR FISHMONGER FOR COD, CUT INTO ROUGHLY 2-INCH CUBES)

2 SPRIGS THYME

2 SPRIGS TARRAGON

½ CUP BUTTER

⅓ CUP ALL-PURPOSE FLOUR

2 ½ CUPS MILK COOKING LIQUID (READ THE METHOD TO FIND OUT WHY)

1 HANDFUL OF ITALIAN PARSLEY LEAVES, CHOPPED

FINELY GRATED ZEST AND JUICE OF 1 LEMON

LEMON WEDGES, TO SERVE

PUMPKIN MASH

1 BUTTERNUT SQUASH (ABOUT 2 POUNDS 10 OUNCES), PEELED, SEEDS REMOVED AND CUT INTO CHUNKS

¾ CUP OLIVE OIL

SEA SALT AND FRESHLY GROUND BLACK PEPPER

1 HANDFUL OF ITALIAN PARSLEY LEAVES, FINELY CHOPPED

FOR THE CRUMBING

1⅓ CUPS ALL-PURPOSE FLOUR

6 FREE-RANGE OR ORGANIC EGGS

¾ CUP MILK

3 ⅔ CUPS DRIED BREAD CRUMBS OR PANKO (JAPANESE) BREAD CRUMBS

VEGETABLE OIL, FOR DEEP-FRYING

This process for making the fish fingers is tiresome, but well worth it. You're basically going to cook the spuds, cook the fish in the milk with the herbs, then combine the milk from cooking the fish with the butter and flour to make a white sauce to bind it all together.

Place the potato in a 8-cup capacity saucepan and fill with cold water until it reaches the brim of the spuds. Bring to a boil, then turn down the heat to medium and cook for 12–14 minutes or until tender. Drain, put the potato back in the pan, place over low heat and allow to dry out for 1–2 minutes. Mash or pass through a mouli. Place in a large bowl and cover with a tea towel until ready to use.

While the potatoes are cooking, place the milk in a separate 8-cup capacity saucepan over medium heat and bring to a simmer, whisking occasionally so the milk does not scorch on the base of the pan. Add the fish, thyme and tarragon, turn down the heat to low and cook for 8 minutes, then take off the heat and leave to cool. Using a slotted spoon, carefully remove the fish and flake into the bowl with the potatoes. Cover the bowl. Pass the milk through a strainer and reserve 2 $\frac{1}{3}$ cups. Discard the rest.

Wash the pan that you cooked the potatoes in, add the butter to the clean pan and melt over low heat. Add the flour and cook for 3 minutes, stirring with a spatula or wooden spoon to mix the flour in. Add $\frac{3}{4}$ cup of the reserved cooking milk and stir until it is fully incorporated, then get a whisk and begin slowly adding the remaining cooking milk, whisking constantly until you have used up all the milk and you have a smooth, lump-free mixture—you just made a white sauce.

Add the white sauce to the potato mixture, along with the parsley and lemon zest and juice, and mix thoroughly. Now you can choose one of two routes. You can mold the mixture into cakes or whatever shape you desire, then chill in the fridge until firm and set before crumbing and cooking. Or you can make fish fingers. If it's the latter, then line a tray (measuring 12 x 8 x 1$\frac{1}{4}$ inches) with parchment paper and spread the mixture evenly over the base, pressing it down until it is all level and smooth. Place in the freezer for 1–2 hours or until it is semi-hard. Remove from the freezer and cut the mixture in half lengthways, then cut each half into 12 fingers, so you should have 24 fingers (about 4 x 1 x 1$\frac{1}{4}$ inches). Place the fingers back in the freezer for another 3 hours or until totally frozen. Freezing the fish fingers will make it easier to crumb and pan fry them.

For the mash, preheat the oven to 425°F. Place the squash in a large roasting tray, coat with $\frac{1}{4}$ cup of the olive oil, season with salt and pepper and roast for 30–35 minutes, shaking a few times during cooking. Take out of the oven and transfer to a large saucepan. Place over low heat, add the remaining olive oil and, using a fork, roughly mash up the squash. Check the seasoning. Just before serving, stir through the parsley.

When you're ready to crumb the fingers, place the flour in a tray or bowl. Whisk the eggs and milk together in a bowl and put to the side. Lastly put the bread crumbs in a bowl or tray.

Working with one fish finger at a time, dip each into the flour, then the eggwash, the bread crumbs, back into the eggwash, finally into the bread crumbs again and place on a tray. (Two fish fingers per person is a good amount. You can refreeze any extra fish fingers after this crumbing stage to save for later.) The crumbing is tedious and messy, so here are my tips: use one hand for the liquid part (eggwash) and the other hand for the dry parts (flour and bread crumbs), or get the missus, old fella or the kids off the couch to come help you. (It could be more fun this way.)

Turn down the oven temperature to 400°F. Heat the oil in a deep-fryer to 350°F or in a deep saucepan (no more than one-third full) and fry the fish fingers, in batches, for 3 minutes or until golden. Drain on paper towels, then place in the oven for 4 minutes or until warm in the center. Serve with the warm mash on the side and lemon wedges for squeezing over.

1 *Add the white sauce to the cooked fish and potato mixture.*

2 *Add parsley and lemon zest and mix well.*

3 *Pour fish and potato mixture into a lined baking sheet.*

4 *Press down firmly until the mixture is level and smooth, then place in freezer.*

5 *Turn fish and potato mixture out onto a board and cut into 24 fingers.*

6 *Dip each fish finger into flour, eggwash, bread crumbs then back into the eggwash and bread crumbs again. Deep fry immediately then finish in the oven (or freeze for later use).*

PUMPKIN & YOGURT PURÉE

MAKES PLENTY BUT NOT TOO MUCH

It's simple but don't be fooled. It's a great purée to accompany many meat and fish dishes.
It's also an easy dip or baby food (but don't go adding the salt or sugar).

1 SMALL SUGAR PUMPKIN, PEELED, SEEDS
REMOVED AND CUT INTO SMALL CHUNKS

3 TABLESPOONS OLIVE OIL

½ TEASPOON UNREFINED LIGHT BROWN SUGAR

⅓ CUP ORGANIC SHEEP'S MILK YOGURT

FINE SEA SALT AND FRESHLY GROUND BLACK PEPPER

Preheat the oven to 400°F. Place the pumpkin in a large roasting tray and coat with the olive oil. Roast for 20–25 minutes or until really soft. A few minutes before you take it out of the oven, sprinkle over the sugar, stir it around and place it back in the oven to finish cooking for about 5 minutes. Transfer to a blender and blitz with the yogurt until a smooth purée. Add salt and pepper and it's ready to go.

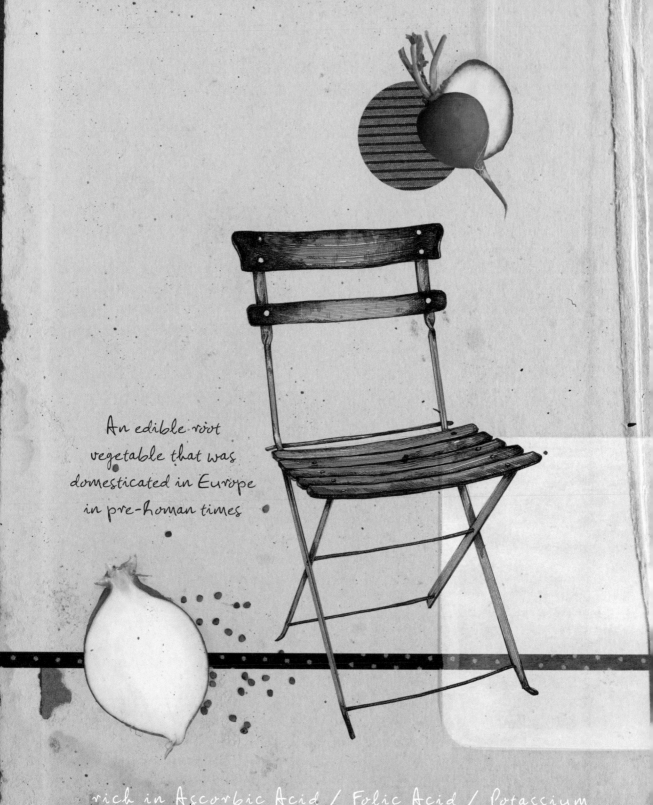

An edible root
vegetable that was
domesticated in Europe
in pre-human times

rich in Ascorbic Acid / Folic Acid / Potassium

VITAMIN C

CAN GERMINATE 3-5 DAYS AFTER SOWING

RADISH

RADISHES ARE VERY VERSATILE
GROWING YEAR ROUND IN ALL BUT
THE COOLEST CLIMATES

(RAPHANUS SATIVUS)

RADISH

On my list of all-time favorite vegetables, at number three, after the carrot and beets, is the radish. So simple. So delicious. I think I really love them for the heat and bite they have. Such a big flavor for what can be such a small vegetable.

PUNCH TO THE PALATE

Radishes are so lovely you really don't need to do anything to them, and the three recipes I've given here are all so light and fresh. They are all about making the radish the star and letting the flavor shine through. They get your tastebuds all excited and leave your mouth zinging for more. And the lovely thing about that is that it stimulates your saliva glands and literally makes your mouth water. When the saliva reaches your stomach, it begins to react with the acids there, getting them boiling and excited for more food. People don't think of vegetables in this way, that a little veggie can evoke that sort of reaction. They tend to think of them only as an accompaniment to meat and not just to be enjoyed for their own sake. And I think that's a bit of a shame. Thankfully, though, the humble radish has enjoyed a great resurgence, and I think it's safe to say the radish has enjoyed the status of being the "it" vegetable for the past few years in the food and restaurant world.

Its reputation and renaissance is certainly not undeserved. I recently had the pleasure of trying radishes with certain styles of Champagne and they match beautifully. What better way to enjoy a French breakfast radish than picking it fresh from the ground, washing and serving it with some beautiful unsalted butter, freshly churned from a local producer and sprinkled with some herb salt? Try the recipe I've included on page 248. It is simple and delicious; radish in one hand, Champagne in the other. I think you'll agree the French really know what they're doing. The other two recipes that I've included are really clean, fresh salads—one simply of heirloom radishes and the other is with figs, walnuts and blue cheese. They are both delicious and really energizing for the palate. Try serving them as a mid-course at your next dinner party and see how they refresh you and stimulate your appetite in anticipation of the next course.

FROM GIZA TO GUMS

Now radishes may have waxed and waned in popularity over the centuries, but humans have been eating them for thousands of years. There is much debate over whether radishes originated in China or ancient Egypt but, whichever is the case, there is evidence that they were being consumed by both civilizations, and being cultivated in Egypt as long as 4,700 years ago. They were also cultivated and enjoyed in ancient Greece and ancient Rome. Records show that they were part of the rations fed to the slaves that built the ancient Pyramids of Giza and they are still very popular right across Asia, even now, where they are mostly enjoyed pickled and preserved.

Radishes have long been praised for their medicinal and digestive properties. They act as a herbal diuretic, assisting in flushing toxins from the body and are supposedly beneficial for the hair, nails, teeth and gums.

You can find radishes in all manner of colors, from bright red to black, from dusky pink to white. The best way to prepare them is dependent on which variety you are working with. I really just love to eat the smallest radishes raw, as they are, with a little salt, as I've mentioned. Or as John Evelyn says, in his book *Aceteria*, published in 1699, radishes are best "eaten alone, with salt only, as conveying their peper [sic] in them."

VARIETIES

Some radishes, like the Asian radish, daikon, are as large as your forearm, while other smaller kinds, like the European radish, are around the size of a raspberry. I've grown many varieties over the years and they've all gone really well from seed. I've found that the timeframe from planting to harvest is about 21–28 days, depending on the variety. And do please grow from seed—I don't see the point of seedlings when radish seeds grow so quickly and fervently anyway.

If you buy a mixed seed lot, you get a lot of different varieties in at once, which is always fun. The only variety I've had trouble growing is the Spanish round. They have a very leathery skin and look almost like a beet from the outside but are white inside. I've been successful with Early Scarlet Globe, which is small, round and red, as the name suggests. The Hailstone (otherwise known as a White Globe) actually looks just like a little turnip and has a mild flavor. The long scarlet can grow up to 6 inches and is just beautiful.

Then there's the Cherry Belle champion, which is a smooth, deep red, and the Sparkler, with its pink top and white tip, which is so lovely and sweet. But my favorite, my absolute favorite variety of all time, would have to be Watermelon. It's white on the outside but cut one and on the inside it has a beautiful pink blush like a watermelon. It is a truly beautiful thing to look at. Its flavor is not as mustardy as the other varieties, but it's still lovely.

GROWING

One tip to extend your harvest is to prepare your garden bed and have it all ready but stagger your planting. Just put in one row every four days otherwise all your radishes will come at once! So if you start planting on a Saturday, plant another row on the Thursday night when you get home from work, then on the following Monday, and continue on like that. Twenty-eight days later, you'll have all the radishes you can eat.

HEIRLOOM RADISHES IN A SALAD

SERVES 4

This salad will do four easily but it's a great number for two with some left over for the next day for lunch. It's the perfect salad to accompany beef. Now I have listed my favorite radishes here for this salad but if you can't get hold of them or the farmer doesn't do variety bunches, pick just one bunch and it will taste just as good (but won't be as visually splendid).

5 FRENCH BREAKFAST RADISHES

5 PLUM PURPLE RADISHES

5 SPARKLER RADISHES

5 WATERMELON RADISHES

1 APPLE (WHATEVER IS BEST IN SEASON), CUT INTO MATCHSTICKS

8 ANCHOVY FILLETS, ROUGHLY CHOPPED

1 LARGE HANDFUL OF ITALIAN PARSLEY LEAVES, CHOPPED

2 TABLESPOONS CHERVIL, CHOPPED

1 TABLESPOON MINT LEAVES, CHOPPED

2 TABLESPOONS HOUSE VINAIGRETTE (SEE PAGE 279)

1 CUP MACHE LETTUCE

5 NASTURTIUM LEAVES

The method is really all in the cutting of the radishes. Take one of each radish and thinly slice on a mandolin and keep in cold water. Take another of each radish and do the same but then cut them into matchsticks and place into the same bowl of water. Cut the rest of the radishes into all sorts of shapes and sizes and set aside. (It feels really weird for me to cut non-uniformly but it's great fun.)

Drain the radishes, place half into a large bowl and add the non-uniformly cut radishes. Add the apple, reserving a little for garnish, along with the anchovies, parsley, chervil and mint. Drizzle over the house vinaigrette so everything is nicely coated. Gently toss through half the mache lettuce, then place into a serving dish. Add the rest of the sliced radishes, apple, remaining mache lettuce and garnish with the nasturtium leaves.

SALAD OF RADISH, FIGS, WALNUTS & BLUE CHEESE

This is probably the most refreshing salad ever. The English cream dressing is great for any leaves that need coating. Don't go overboard, though. There's no need to drown the leaves. Add only enough dressing to coat the leaves as a Caesar dressing would coat romaine lettuce.

1 BUNCH RADISHES (MIXED HEIRLOOM VARIETIES IF POSSIBLE), TOPPED AND TAILED

3 RIPE LARGE FIGS

1 SMALL BUTTER LETTUCE, LEAVES SEPARATED AND WASHED

1 SMALL GREEN OR RED OAK LETTUCE, LEAVES SEPARATED AND WASHED

3 CUPS WILD ARUGULA, PICKED AND WASHED

¼ BUNCH MINT, LEAVES PICKED AND FINELY CHOPPED

½ CUP WALNUTS, ROUGHLY CHOPPED

3 ½ OUNCES ROQUEFORT CHEESE OR OTHER CREAMY BLUE-STYLE CHEESE

2 TABLESPOONS CORIANDER SEEDS, TOASTED AND ROUGHLY CRUSHED

ENGLISH CREAM DRESSING

3 TABLESPOONS HOT ENGLISH MUSTARD

3 TABLESPOONS CHARDONNAY VINEGAR

1 CUP LIGHT CREAM

2 PINCHES OF FINE SEA SALT

2 PINCHES OF WHITE SUGAR

For the English cream dressing, whisk the mustard and vinegar together in a bowl. Whisk in the cream, then the salt and sugar. Set aside.

Thickly slice the radishes and place in a bowl. Slice the figs into 6 wedges and add to the bowl. Add the salad leaves, mint and some walnuts and crumble over some of the cheese but reserve a little for garnishing. Mix in just enough of the English dressing to coat the leaves. Arrange the salad on a plate, scatter over the coriander seeds and remaining walnuts and cheese.

RADISHES SIMPLY WITH BUTTER & HERB SALT

SERVES MANY OR 1

Where does history start and end? The French from Normandy and Brittany will tell you that this dish is theirs. Then you get some old chap from good old England talking and he'd tell you that the French don't know what they're on about and this is obviously British in heritage. Personally, I couldn't give two hoots where this came from but this is the most simple and beautiful thing ever—a freshly picked radish covered in soft unsalted butter with a good sprinkle of salt on it. Butter and salt—great for the heart, yeah! At least there are some radishes involved.

1 BUNCH RADISHES (I'D USE THE FRENCH
BREAKFAST OR CHAMPION VARIETY)

GOOD-QUALITY UNSALTED BUTTER, SOFTENED

HERB SALT (SEE PAGE 279)

I highly recommend growing your own or buy the freshest available from a market stall. It's important to have that hard radish texture that bursts with heat and earthy flavor that is so unique to radishes. All you have to do is simply wash and dry the radishes, cut in half, place on a wooden board with a little pot of the butter and a small mound of the salt as well. Serve as a canapé or enjoy just by yourself with a glass of cider while reading a book.

The word "tomato" comes from the
Nahuati word tomati, literally
"the swelling fruit"

sugo, passata, tomato paste,
sauces, ketchups, chutneys, stews

SUN + SUN + SUN

BIG
RAINBOW hungarian heart TIGERELLA ISIS CANDY
GREEN ZEBRA BLACK CHERRY lemon drop BLACK RUSSIAN

TOMATO

The tomato came from South America
courtesy of the Spanish colonizers,
and via Spain to the rest of Europe.

TOMATO

I close my eyes and smell that vibrant scent of the tomato, it's unmistakable—
zingy, earthy and fruity. It's probably one smell everyone in the world could recognize.

MY GRANDAD'S TRUE LOVE

My Grandad Tom gave me my love for tomatoes. At the back of his house, in a small mining village called Barnsley, was an oasis of things that had been grown to eat, and the two masterpieces in his greenhouse were the passion fruit flower (which he always wore on his lapel when he used to go to the club on Friday nights to impress the ladies) and the glorious tomato. He grew them everywhere—in the greenhouse, in the garden, in the house, even in the coal shed. I guess it was him that gave me a love of gardening, passed down through my own father, "Wilkie" Snr.

Gardening back in my grandad's day wasn't like it is today where we find ourselves doing it mainly as a hobby. For him, with certain produce not being widely available, especially during the war, growing your own produce was a necessity so you could have the vegetables of the season at hand.

I've only come around in the past two years not to eat a tomato out of season. I will use the canned variety instead as I believe they are a good product, with the tomatoes captured at their peak, and also because preserving things for use when they are out of season is how we are able to survive. The varieties available to us year round taste so watery, smell of chemicals and, not to mention, are so much more expensive. A tomato at its peak is such a delight, especially now that we have so many heirloom varietals re-emerging and making their way into our supermarkets and nurseries.

A TOMATO BY ANY OTHER NAME IS JUST AS SWEET

In fact, when you think about it, tomatoes are everywhere. And it's hard to imagine any Western cuisine without them, especially Italian. Whether they are used in sugo, tomato paste, sauces, ketchups, chutneys, stews, fresh, cooked, canned or bottled, tomatoes are a staple of the modern diet. It's surprizing then to discover that the tomato was viewed with huge suspicion by most when it was first introduced. It came from South America courtesy of the Spanish colonizers in the early 1500s, and then via Spain through to Italy and the rest of Europe, including the UK. It took the general population a long time to warm to them, and while they were always around, they only increased in popularity after the mid-1700s, following the fashion of importing delicacies from the continent.

There were a few reasons for people to be apprehensive, even if they were all ultimately incorrect. It started with the name. They were known as "love apples," and were grown as an ornament, something that a man would present to his lady as a token of love. There was also a yellow variety (much more common then than now) whose fruit supposedly resembled the biblical mandrake plant, long thought to have aphrodisiac qualities. Hence the Italian title "pomo d'oro" or "golden apple."

They were also thought to be very bad for the digestion, the skins said to stick to the lining of the stomach, and many doctors warned against eating them. Again this refers back to their name, this time their scientific one, *Lycopersicon esculentum*, which translates as "wolf peach." The "peach" part is understandable due to its shape, but "wolf" was because of their relation to the deadly nightshade family and the assumption that tomatoes, too, must be poisonous.

There is a persistent myth of how they came to be accepted as safe for consumption in America, and that was when, in 1820, one Colonel Johnson stood on the steps of the courthouse in Salem and proceeded to eat an entire basket of raw tomatoes. A large crowd gathered in anticipation of seeing him die slowly, and were probably really disappointed when he didn't!

GROWING

For my part, there's something so great about growing your own tomatoes. There's such a variety to choose from, for starters, including all sizes, shapes and colors. Red, yellow, green, striped, cherry, pear, plum, the list just goes on. I do know, however, that some people find them quite intimidating to grow. All I can say is give it a go, and you'll be pleasantly surprised. They are a self-pollinating plant, which basically means they can reproduce all on their own. So don't be surprised if some pop up in your compost. You can always pull the little fellows out and plant them in a pot or garden bed. If they can survive on their own, imagine how well they will do with a bit of love, food and water. They really love warm weather, quite a lot of sun, and well-drained soil with a heap of compost and manure added. If they are the taller-growing varieties, you will need to tie them to a stake for support as they grow. One little tip I discovered too: they are very sensitive to tobacco, and will wilt if touched with a hand that has held a cigarette. Strange but true.

A great companion for the tomato—both in eating and growing—is beautiful sweet basil. Dot a few of these in between your tomatoes and come harvest time you will have the makings of a lovely fresh, light panzanella salad (see page 256) or as I like to call it, "summer in a bowl." I think even Grandad Tom would approve.

MY FRESH TOMATO STEW FOR ALL SORTS OF THINGS

→ *MAKES ABOUT 4 CUPS*

We all have a fail-safe recipe that lets us, at the last moment, pull a rabbit out of the hat. During the summer months, this is mine. It's great with pasta, steak or chicken, brilliant on eggplant or with marinated sardines, or can be used as a base for Bolognese.

3 TABLESPOONS EXTRA VIRGIN OLIVE OIL

6 TOMATOES (MIXED HEIRLOOMS PREFERABLY), ROUGHLY CHOPPED

3 SHALLOTS, SLICED

2 GARLIC CLOVES, SLICED

1 OUNCE SALTED BABY CAPERS, RINSED

14 TURNS OF BLACK PEPPER FROM A MILL

1 ½ TABLESPOONS RED WINE VINEGAR

1 PINCH OF FINE SEA SALT

1 PINCH OF WHITE SUGAR

1 SMALL HANDFUL OF BASIL LEAVES, SHREDDED

1 SMALL HANDFUL ITALIAN PARSLEY LEAVES, SHREDDED

Heat a large skillet at least 10 inches in diameter over medium heat. Add the olive oil and heat for 1 minute, then add the tomato, shallot and garlic and cook out for 5 minutes. Add the capers and pepper, turn the heat to high, stir in the vinegar and ⅓ cup of water, bring to a boil, then turn down the heat and cook for 5–7 minutes or until the tomato has started to break down. Add the salt and sugar, take off the heat and add the herbs. Kapow! It's ready.

MY VERSION OF PANZANELLA: TOMATOES, BURRATA, BASIL, MIGAS & GREEN OLIVES

SERVES 4 AS ENTRÉE
OR AS A MAIN-DISH SALAD

There can't be any other salad that shows off summer as much as a panzanella. My take is simply lots of different tomatoes, basil, green olives, some old bread that has been dipped in a smoked paprika oil and dried to make "migas" and burrata, which is a small ball of fresh mozzarella with a drop of seasoned cream in the center. If you can't find it, substitute with good-quality fresh mozza.

LEMON AND VINCOTTO DRESSING

JUICE OF 3 LEMONS

3 TABLESPOONS VINCOTTO

1 TABLESPOON DIJON MUSTARD

1 CUP OLIVE OIL

3 TABLESPOONS CHARDONNAY VINEGAR

FINE SEA SALT AND FRESHLY GROUND BLACK PEPPER

MIGAS

7 OUNCES STALE CIABATTA BREAD

¾ CUP OLIVE OIL

1 TEASPOON SMOKED PAPRIKA

TO ASSEMBLE

ABOUT 8 MIXED HEIRLOOM TOMATOES (SEE NOTE), CUT INTO ANY SHAPES YOU LIKE

½ CUP GREEN OLIVES, CRUSHED AND PITTED

¼ BUNCH BASIL, BABY LEAVES PICKED

2 RED ASIAN SHALLOTS, FINELY DICED

2 BURRATA, ROUGHLY CHOPPED

SEA SALT AND FRESHLY GROUND BLACK PEPPER

For the lemon and vincotto dressing, whisk all the ingredients together in a bowl.

For the migas, preheat the oven to 350°F and line a baking sheet with parchment paper. Slice the ciabatta into thick, long fingers. Whisk together the oil and paprika in a shallow bowl, then dip in the bread and place on the tray. Bake for 9–13 minutes or until crisp on the outside but still a little soft on the inside.

To assemble, marinate the sliced tomatoes in a little of the dressing for 20 minutes. Arrange onto a serving plate or bowl. Toss most of the olives and basil and all the shallot and migas together in a bowl, then arrange over the sliced tomatoes in any way you like really. Dress with a little more dressing, then scatter over the burrata. Season with salt and pepper, then top with the remaining basil and olives.

Note My favorite heirloom varieties include: Wapsipinicon Peach, Tigerella, Jaune Flamme, Brown Berry, Green Zebra, Purple Russian, Beam's Yellow Pear, Black Russian, Tommy Toe and Black Krim.

PICKLED GREEN TOMATOES

FILLS A 6 CUP JAR

It's up to you really how you go about selecting your green tomatoes. You may choose the Green Zebra variety or tomatillos, but for me I usually either pickle green tomatoes from the start of the season (the juvenile green tomatoes that have blossomed early) or from the end of the season (the immature ones that will not ripen). Whatever you choose, here is a fail-safe recipe for putting green tomatoes to good use. I like to use the pickled tomatoes in any form of toasted sandwich, in a salad or with a slice of cheese.

ABOUT 8 GREEN TOMATOES, THINLY SLICED

6 SHALLOTS, THINLY SLICED

3 LARGE GARLIC CLOVES, THINLY SLICED

3 TABLESPOONS FINE SEA SALT

1 SMALL GREEN CHILI, THINLY SLICED

4 CUPS WHITE WINE VINEGAR

⅔ CUP EXTRA VIRGIN OLIVE OIL

2 TEASPOONS CORIANDER SEEDS

2 TEASPOONS CRUSHED BLACK PEPPERCORNS

Place the tomato, shallot, garlic and salt in a large bowl and leave to sit for 5 minutes. This will bring out the moisture. Drain, then place the tomato in a large sterilized glass jar.

Place the remaining ingredients and 1 ⅓ cups of water in a large saucepan and bring to a boil, then pour over the tomato. Allow to cool, then seal with a lid and store for at least 1 week before using. Store in the fridge after opening for up to 2 months.

SMOKED TOMATO & GOAT CHEESE GOUGÈRES

→ *MAKES 20 SMALL GOUGÈRES*

It may seem like a lot of fiddling around but these simple yet delicious canapés rock the kasbah. If you can't buy smoked tomatoes, I have included a way to smoke your own tomatoes on page 277 —it's simple to do and I'm sure you will find yourself adding them to all sorts of incarnations; try them with a poached egg and some salted zucchini (see page 268). If you don't want to go to the trouble, then a little cheat's method (but you didn't hear it from me) is to peel and roast some tomatoes and sprinkle them with smoked salt. It's a good substitute, especially for this recipe.

FILLING

3 SMOKED TOMATOES, FLESH ONLY

7 OUNCES SOFT, FRESH GOAT CHEESE OR FROMAGE BLANC

SEA SALT AND FRESHLY GROUND BLACK PEPPER

GOUGÈRES

3 TABLESPOONS MILK

1 ½ TABLESPOONS BUTTER, DICED

1 PINCH OF FINE SEA SALT

1 PINCH OF WHITE SUGAR

½ CUP ALL-PURPOSE FLOUR

2 FREE-RANGE OR ORGANIC EGGS

⅔ CUP FINELY GRATED PARMESAN

1 FREE-RANGE OR ORGANIC EGG YOLK, WHISKED WITH A FORK

For the gougères, preheat the oven to 400°F and line a baking sheet with parchment paper.

Place 3 tablespoons of water, the milk and butter in a saucepan and bring to a boil, then turn down the heat to low, add the salt, sugar and flour and, using a wooden spoon, whip until a smooth paste forms. Keep cooking out for 4–5 minutes, then take off the heat. Using the wooden spoon, beat in the eggs, then two-thirds of the Parmesan. You can at this point transfer the mixture to a food processor or to the bowl of an electric mixer to beat until cooled or just beat by hand.

Place the cooled mixture into a frosting bag fitted with a plain medium nozzle and pipe small rounds (about the size of a macadamia nut) onto the tray. Lightly brush with the whisked egg yolk and sprinkle with the remaining Parmesan. Bake for 12–18 minutes or until risen and golden. Place onto a wire rack and, using a small knife, make a hole, in the bases, only large enough so a small piping nozzle will fit into it.

For the smoked tomato and goat cheese filling, blitz together the smoked tomato flesh and goat cheese and season with salt and pepper. Transfer to a icing bag fitted with a small nozzle and pipe a little of the filling into the gougères. Flash in the oven to warm through, then serve immediately. There will be excess filling to serve on the side to dip into if you wish.

TOMATO KASUNDI

FILLS TWO 4-CUP CAPACITY JARS

*British cuisine owes so much to the flavors of India and, on behalf of us Brits,
I say thank you. Especially for a nice cup of tea and this great spicy tomato pickle sauce.*

4 ½ OUNCE PIECE OF FRESH GINGER, PEELED AND CHOPPED

2 ½ OUNCES GARLIC

¾ OUNCE GREEN CHILIS, HALVED AND SEEDS REMOVED

¾ CUP VEGETABLE OIL

⅓ CUP BLACK MUSTARD SEEDS

½ OUNCE GROUND TURMERIC

2 OUNCES GROUND CUMIN

PINCH CHILI POWDER

2 POUNDS 10 ½ OUNCES CANNED CHOPPED TOMATOES

3 TEASPOONS FINE SEA SALT

1 ¼ CUPS APPLE CIDER VINEGAR

¾ CUP UNREFINED LIGHT BROWN SUGAR

Mince the ginger, garlic and chili in a food processor until a smooth paste forms.

Heat the vegetable oil in a heavy-bottomed 12-cup capacity saucepan over medium heat. Gently toast all the spices for 5 minutes to release their natural oils.

Add the ginger paste to the pan and cook for 5 minutes. Add the tomatoes, salt, vinegar and sugar, bring to a boil, then reduce to a simmer and cook for 1–1 ½ hours. When the oil has come to the top and it looks like a curry sauce, it is ready. Take off the heat, and pour into sterilized preserving jars with lids. Keep for 4 weeks before using to give the flavors time to mature. This sauce will keep for a good year in a cool dark place. Once opened, store in the fridge and use within 3 months.

WHILE EASY TO GROW, ZUCCHINI REQUIRES
PLENTIFUL BEES FOR POLLINATION.

Good old zucchini has many aliases: courgette,
summer squash and marrow. Eat them raw, baked,
grilled or fried, in salad, soups and sautés not
to mention cakes breads and muffins.

BLACK BEAUTY, BLANCO, LUNGO CYLINDRIC
COSTATA, GOLDEN YELLOW, COOL WHITE

ZUCCHINI

ANCESTRY IS THE AMERICAS
BUT DEVELOPED IN ITALY

Needs to be regularly harvested
to encourage continuous cropping

(CUCURBITA PEPO)

ZUCCHINI

Good old zucchini has many aliases, depending on where you are and where you grew up.
In the UK, they are courgettes, in some parts of America they are known as summer squash,
and they can also go by the name marrow, depending on their size. It can all get a little confusing.

SALTING IS KEY

As a young chef there were a lot of things I disliked. Maybe it was youthfulness, ignorance or even (gulp) arrogance, but there were a lot of vegetables I "hated." In the early days of my cooking career, I will admit that I found zucchini to be watery and pretty tasteless. And still now I find myself reverting to those old ways. It's so easy to react like a five year old, sticking your tongue out and saying, "Uck!" when thinking of zucchini. But somehow, somewhere, something changed. Maybe it was just that my palate matured but, as a general rule, I really do love it now. I think it was the discovery of salting the zucchini for a few minutes before cooking or eating raw that has helped me to remove that earlier memory of a watery vegetable. In fact, this is what I now do for the majority of my recipes involving zucchini. This is a simple device to get rid of excess moisture within the vegetable, and it also creates a really lovely, different texture.

USES

What we now know as the zucchini is a variety that was developed and warmly embraced in Italy. Like many things, Columbus brought the zucchini back to Europe in his luggage from the South Americas, and it has been widely adopted ever since. It took somewhat longer to reach the UK and Australia, the first real introduction was from the wonderful Elizabeth David in her classic cookbook *Mediterranean Food*, which was first published in 1950. She removed the mystery from these then little-known vegetables and encouraged their widespread growth and use. And we should all be grateful she did—they are so versatile. You can salt them and eat them raw, you can eat them baked, broiled, pickled, grated or fried, in salad, soups and sautés, not to mention cakes, breads and muffins. They are central to Italian cuisine. After all, what would a ratatouille or minestrone be without zucchini? They are treated just as reverentially in the Deep South where, naturally, they are coated in batter and deep-fried to make delicious zucchini fritters.

I haven't included any sweet recipes in here but, if you have a flick through a few old cookbooks, I'll guarantee you'll come across some amazing cake recipes that involve the humble zuc too. This may be because they were generally a cheap vegetable and, perhaps, therefore within the budget of the frugal hausfrau. But also, once people started using them, it was discovered that zucchini contain a lot of natural moisture, making them a great addition to slices and cakes to stop them from drying out.

And it's great for kids too. If they say they don't like it, just don't tell 'em it's in there. They'll never know otherwise! (That is an excellent little cheat to sneak more veggies into kids' diets, actually. Zucchini is great because its flavor is so mild, you can put it in pretty much any dish—a favorite pasta sauce, for instance, and they won't pick it. Secret vitamins! Ha ha!)

I'm sure you all know that the flower of the zucchini can also be eaten. Stuffed zucchini flowers were all the rage in restaurants and magazines there for a bit—I'll even put my hand up and say I got caught up in the moment and did a couple of versions, although now I'm not entirely sure why. Don't get me wrong, they are quite lovely, and I'm not against using the flower, but if I do use it now I will use the male variety. Plants contain "male" and "female" parts for reproduction and zucchini is no different. If you look at the plant itself, the male is the flower with a very long thin stalk. The female is the fruit producer and her flower will have a small zucchini attached. You still get the visual effect and flavor from using the male, but you can still grow your zucchini to full size also.

GROWING

And, speaking of growing, I am very proud to say it's one of the few veggies I have triumphantly and successfully grown. But there is a secret to getting your vine to behave and that is to be absolutely vicious with your pruning shears. It's all about tough love. You have to be the one in control and don't be scared to keep cutting it back, because it will spread everywhere, in very similar fashion to a pumpkin vine, and it will do so very quickly. From one plant you should get at least 20 zucchini a year. More than enough for you and your neighbors too I should imagine.

But don't just limit yourself to good old green. Like most plants there are many really lovely lesser-known varieties out there. I like the little fat white zucs, myself. They tend to be very sweet and delicate. Yellow ones are nice for their vibrant color, but they do discolor quite quickly if you don't treat them gently. They'll hold up quite well in a brown paper bag in the fridge.

The key to zucchini selection is the younger and smaller the better. As they get older they will become bitter and full of water and seeds. Harvest them no bigger than the diameter of a golf ball, salt them before use and that's it.

SALTED & LEMONED RAW ZUCCHINI, FROMAGE BLANC & GRATED ALMOND

SERVES 4 AS A SALAD TO SHARE

A simple yet delicious salad that is great on its own, but also rocks with a little sandwich on the side. You can omit the salmon roe, if you wish, but the texture of the roe really enhances the dish.

4 SMALLISH GREEN ZUCCHINI

2 NOT-SO-HEALTHY PINCHES OF SEA SALT

JUICE OF 1 LEMON

⅓ CUP EXTRA VIRGIN OLIVE OIL

3 TABLESPOONS FINELY CHOPPED ITALIAN PARSLEY

1 CUP TORN BASIL LEAVES

1 TOMATO, QUARTERED, SEEDS REMOVED AND THINLY SLICED

3 ½ OUNCES FROMAGE BLANC (USE FROMAGE FRAIS IF YOU WANT)

5 ORGANIC RAW ALMONDS

3 TABLESPOONS SALMON ROE (OPTIONAL)

FRESHLY GROUND BLACK PEPPER

Thinly slice the zucchini on a mandoline into ribbons, then slice, using a sharp knife, into thin strips. Place in a colander, toss with the salt and let stand for 3 minutes.

Rinse off the salt and pat dry with paper towels. Place in a large bowl, add the lemon juice and olive oil and let stand again for 3 minutes. Pour off any excess liquid. Mix through the herbs and tomato and transfer to a serving plate. Spoon over the fromage blanc, then finely grate the almonds, using a Microplane, over the salad. Spoon over liberal amounts of the salmon roe and finish with some pepper.

ZUCCHINI-WRAPPED JOHN DORY, TOMATO, PINE NUTS & STEAMED ZUCCHINI FLOWERS

→ SERVES 2

2 ZUCCHINI

FINE SEA SALT, FOR SPRINKLING

2 X 4½ OUNCES JOHN DORY, SEA BASS OR TURBOT FILLETS, SKIN REMOVED

2 TABLESPOONS OLIVE OIL, PLUS EXTRA FOR DRIZZLING

1 MEDIUM POTATO, PEELED, DICED AND BOILED UNTIL TENDER

1 TOMATO, QUARTERED, SEEDS REMOVED AND FINELY DICED

2 TABLESPOONS CURRANTS, SOAKED IN WARM WATER, THEN DRAINED

1 TABLESPOON PINE NUTS, TOASTED

3 TABLESPOONS WHITE WINE

1 TABLESPOON BASIL LEAVES, FINELY CHOPPED

1 TABLESPOON CHIVES, FINELY CHOPPED

SEA SALT AND FRESHLY GROUND BLACK PEPPER

6 ZUCCHINI FLOWERS (MALE OR FEMALE)

JUICE OF 1 LEMON

2¾ OUNCES FETA CHEESE (OPTIONAL)

Preheat the oven to 350°F.

Take one zucchini, top and tail it, then thinly slice on a mandoline lengthways. You should get 12 good long strips. Lay these side by side on a tray, sprinkle with the salt and let stand for 8 minutes to draw out the moisture, which will make it easier to wrap the fish in. Rinse off the salt. Layer 6 slices lengthways side by side slightly overlapping onto a tea towel and pat dry. Repeat with the remaining slices. Now a John Dory has three pieces in one fillet. Fold the pieces lengthways like a little parcel, then place in the middle of the zucchini ribbons. Using the tea towel as a guide, carefully lift and wrap the zucchini around the fish, then place, seam side down, onto a tray.

Heat a skillet over high heat, add 3 teaspoons of the olive oil and place the zucchini-wrapped fish, seam side down, into the pan and pan fry for 2 minutes. Turn over, turn down the heat and fry the presentation side for 3 minutes. Carefully take out of the pan and place on a baking sheet. Wash the pan.

Now dice the remaining zucchini (and any left-over fish scraps). Place the clean pan over high heat, add the rest of the oil and heat for 1–2 minutes. When hot, add the diced zucchini and cook for 2 minutes. Turn down the heat to medium, add the potato and tomato and cook for 2 minutes. Add the currants, pine nuts and wine, turn up the heat to high and cook until the liquid is reduced by half. Take off the heat, add the herbs and season with salt and pepper. Put to the side.

Put the tray of zucchini-wrapped John Dory in the oven for 10 minutes. Steam the zucchini flowers for 2–3 minutes. To serve, divide the zucchini mixture between plates. Squeeze the lemon juice over the fish. Place on the plates, lay the zucchini flowers on top, drizzle with olive oil and crumble over the feta.

ZUCCHINI & OLIVE DRESSING

MAKES 1½ CUPS

This is my version of a tapenade but with a little twist. It not only goes great with simple boiled potatoes, all white fish and on steamed vegetables but it also makes a nice dressing for salad leaves.

3–4 TABLESPOONS OLIVE OIL

2 SMALL ZUCCHINI,
CUT INTO PINKY-NAIL-SIZED CUBES

2 GARLIC CLOVES, THINLY SLICED

2 TABLESPOONS CHARDONNAY VINEGAR

⅔ CUP BLACK OLIVES, PITTED

2 ANCHOVY FILLETS (OPTIONAL)

SEA SALT AND FRESHLY GROUND BLACK PEPPER

10 BASIL LEAVES, FINELY CHOPPED

Heat 3 tablespoons of the olive oil in a skillet over medium heat. Add the zucchini and garlic and sauté until lightly brown and softened. Turn down the heat and deglaze the pan with the vinegar. Take off the heat and divide the mixture into two batches. Reserve one-half for later. Place the other in a blender along with the olives, anchovies and remaining olive oil (if you like) and season with salt and pepper. Blitz for 30–40 seconds or until a smooth paste forms. Pour into a bowl and fold in the reserved zucchini mixture and the basil. Add a little more olive oil if it needs to be a little wetter, check the salt and pepper levels, then it's ready to go. It will keep in the fridge for up to 1 week.

BASICS

PRESERVED LEMON DRESSING

This dressing can be used for any salad leaves where you need to coat the leaves, for example butter or iceberg lettuce, but also works well mixed in couscous.

3 PRESERVED LEMONS, PEEL ONLY WITH THE WHITE PITH REMOVED

¾ CUP EXTRA VIRGIN OLIVE OIL

3 TABLESPOONS CHARDONNAY VINEGAR

SALT AND PEPPER

Blitz the preserved lemon peel in a food processor, add the olive oil and vinegar, season with salt and pepper and pulse to combine. This will keep in the fridge for up to 1 month.

TARRAGON EMULSION

MAKES ABOUT 1 CUP

This makes an amazing salad dressing for all sorts of things.

1 ½ TABLESPOONS DIJON MUSTARD

3 TABLESPOONS CHARDONNAY VINEGAR

2 TABLESPOONS TARRAGON VINEGAR

⅓ CUP GRAPESEED OIL

2 TEASPOONS CHOPPED TARRAGON

Whisk together the mustard, vinegars and oil until emulsified, then stir through the tarragon.

COOKING GRAINS & FRESH & DRIED BEANS

DRIED BEANS

Soak ½ cup of dried beans in 2 cups of water for 24 hours. Drain and place in a saucepan with 6 cups of water, bring to a boil and cook for 40–45 minutes or until tender. Drain and use as directed in the recipe. Makes 2 cups.

CHICKPEAS (GARBANZOS)

Soak ½ cup of chickpeas in 2 cups of water for 24 hours. Drain and place in a saucepan with 6 cups of water, bring to a boil and cook for 35–45 minutes or until tender. Drain and use as directed in the recipe. Makes 2½ cups.

QUINOA

Bring 4 cups of water to the boil in a saucepan. Add ½ cup quinoa and cook for 10–12 minutes or until the center spiral pops out. Drain and use as directed in the recipe. Makes 1½ cups.

PEARL BARLEY, SPELT OR FARRO

Place ½ cup of pearl barley, spelt or farro in a saucepan with 6 cups of water, bring to a boil and cook for 22–26 minutes or until tender. Drain and use as directed in the recipe. Makes 1½ cups.

FREGOLA

Bring 4 cups of water to the boil in a saucepan. Add ½ cup fregola and cook for 8–10 minutes or until tender. Drain and use as directed in the recipe. Makes 1½ cups.

LENTILS

Rinse ½ cup of lentils and place in a saucepan with 4 cups of water. Bring to a boil and cook for 22–26 minutes or until tender. Drain and use as directed in the recipe. Makes 1½ cups.

FREEKAH (CRACKED WHEAT)

Place ½ cup of freekah in a saucepan with 4 cups of water, bring to a boil and cook for 18–22 minutes or until tender. Drain and use as directed in the recipe. Makes 1½ cups.

A GUIDE TO SMOKED TOMATOES

At Pope Joan I buy all my things salted, cured and smoked from two great men: David Snr and
David Jnr, grand fellows from the midlands in the UK, who have set up shop in Melbourne.
They do all sorts of smoking for me, from bacon and salmon to eggs and yogurt, but it is their
smoked tomatoes that rock. Here is David Jnr's method for homemade cold-smoked tomatoes.
Remember, this all depends on how many tomatoes you smoke and the trays you have
at home, so it's not really a recipe but a guide to how to smoke them.

A 8-CUP CAPACITY POT

RIPE PLUM TOMATOES

A BOWL FILLED WITH ICY COLD WATER

SEA SALT, FRESHLY GROUND BLACK
PEPPER AND SUPERFINE SUGAR

A WIRE RACK

A GOOD HANDFUL OF SMOKING CHIPS

A SKILLET

A ROASTING TRAY THAT THE WIRE RACK FITS IN

SOME FOIL

Preheat the oven to 450°F.

Fill the pot with 4 cups of water, place over high heat and bring to a boil. Take out the white core of the
tomatoes, place the tomatoes into the water, leave in for 10 seconds, then scoop out and submerge the
tomatoes in the icy cold water. This is called blanching. Now peel the tomatoes, rub with the salt, pepper
and sugar, then place on the wire rack.

Put the smoking chips in the skillet and smoke on the stovetop. Once smoking, add to the roasting tray, put
the rack over the top, then cover with foil and pierce 5 holes in the foil. Place in the oven for 5 minutes. Take
out straight away, then place the tray in the fridge until the tomatoes are cool. You may need to put a tea
towel under the tray in the fridge to prevent it from melting your fridge shelves (David left that part out,
but don't worry he's from Birmingham). Really, that's it. And you have smoked tomatoes.

ALMOND & ORANGE SPICED CRUMB

MAKES 1 CUP

FINELY GRATED ZEST OF 2 ORANGES

1 TEASPOON COARSELY GROUND BLACK PEPPER

2 JUNIPER BERRIES

½ CUP ORGANIC BLANCHED ALMONDS

2 TEASPOONS SEA SALT

2 TEASPOONS UNREFINED LIGHT BROWN SUGAR

Preheat the oven to 350°F.

Place the orange zest on a plate lined with a piece of parchment paper and put into the microwave set on defrost for about 12 minutes (depending on the power of your microwave). The zest should be completely dried out but it should retain its color and scent.

Place the dried zest, pepper and juniper berries in a mortar and grind to dust.

Roast the almonds in the oven for 4–8 minutes or until they are just tanning, then add to the mortar. Pound the almonds until they are about the size of a grain of rice, then stir through the salt and brown sugar.

Note I use this spice mix in my blanched white asparagus with ricotta and Belgian endive (see page 4) but it's also delicious on numerous other vegetables, such as broccoli and leeks, or try a little on a roasted chicken or a simple poached fish dish. It will keep for up to 6 months in a tightly sealed jar in your pantry.

DUKKA

MAKES 1 CUP

Do you know why it's better to toast spices? To release the natural oils within them, which promotes their beautiful aroma and taste. The best way to do this is in a flat-based skillet over low heat, shaking the pan all the time. As soon as you see any signs of smoke or steam coming from the spices, take the pan off the heat and tip the spices into a bowl to cool quickly. They are now ready to use.

⅔ CUP HAZELNUTS

2 TEASPOONS WHITE PEPPERCORNS

1 TABLESPOON CORIANDER SEEDS, TOASTED

1 TABLESPOON SESAME SEEDS, TOASTED

2 TEASPOONS GROUND CUMIN, TOASTED

1 ½ TABLESPOONS SEA SALT

1 TABLESPOON UNREFINED LIGHT BROWN SUGAR

Preheat the oven to 350°F. Roast the hazelnuts for 5–10 minutes. Place in a tea towel and rub off the skins while still warm.

Place the hazelnuts in a mortar and grind to break up, then add the peppercorns and coriander seeds and grind to a milled pepper consistency. Now stir through the rest of the ingredients and store in an airtight container until needed. This will store well for a good few months.

HERB SALT

MAKES ABOUT 2 CUPS

If herb salt was a lady it would be Rita Hayworth: timeless, elegant and beautifully tasty. This must become one of your kitchen pantry basics—on hand, all the time, to give that extra bit of finesse to a dish.

⅔ CUP VEGETABLE OIL

5 ⅔ OUNCES ROSEMARY, OREGANO AND SAGE LEAVES

⅔ CUP SEA SALT

Gently heat the oil in a shallow saucepan over medium heat to 325°F. Add the herbs and deep fry for 7–10 minutes or until crispy. Turn off the heat and scoop out the herbs onto a tray lined with lots of paper towels. Take the herbs off the towel and dry again on a tea towel. Place into a mortar with the salt and finely crush all together. Keep in an airtight container for up to 6 months and use just as you would any normal salt.

Note Ever wondered what to do with those left-over herbs like parsley and basil that are just withering at the bottom of your fridge. Hey presto, here you go. Just use them up to make this salt to avoid wasting them. When you use soft-leaved herbs gently fry them for a little less time, 3–4 minutes, say.

HOUSE VINAIGRETTE

MAKES 4 CUPS

This is my basic dressing for many salads. Once made, store in empty washed-out wine bottles, topped with a cork and it will keep for a few months.

2 CUPS EXTRA VIRGIN OLIVE OIL

1 ½ CUPS SUNFLOWER OIL

⅓ CUP CHARDONNAY VINEGAR

⅓ CUP TARRAGON VINEGAR

10 TURNS OF WHITE PEPPER FROM A MILL

1 PINCH OF SALT

3 GARLIC CLOVES, LIGHTLY CRUSHED

4 SPRIGS TARRAGON

Whisk everything together and pour into bottles. Make sure you give it a good shake before using.

INDEX

ACKNOWLEDGEMENTS

A massive sincere thank you to:

Family and friends from near and far shores.

Mum, Dad, Lucy, Richard and my little niece, Molly Rebecca. To all my grandparents, aunties and uncles with us and past. I am today because of your guidance, knowledge and love. And yes you too Uncle K. To Leah and Struan for making my new family here in Australia such a loved place to be.

My dearest friends Jeff and Jacq, Nick and Tara, Pete-Pete, Ben and Larissa: without support and friendship dreams cannot be made, and to all my staff at Pope Joan who make owning a business so much fun and so pleasurable.

To friends and old bosses of the cooking world, you know who you are, to whom I am ever indebted for sharing your passions with me and pointing me in the right direction, but I have to say special thank yous to Michael Taylor for nurturing me and setting off my passion for food, to Martin Wishart for showing me a new world that would make all things possible and to Andrew McConnell for guiding me to take my blinkers off and showing me all that the world of food and its many cultures has to offer.

I could not do a thank you without mentioning some people from Circa, the Prince: Lisa and John Van Haandel, Rosanne and Jenni for believing in me to run an amazing business, David Moyle for the early days and Jake and all the kitchen team for their dedication to me.

To the best team to put together a book and believing in me that we could do it, starting with my dear friend Brydie, who is like my little sister, thank you for your words that make me sound much better; to Stacey for her exquisite drawings; to Paul and Rachel—words can't describe your work; to Madame Jacqui Melville for her amazing photos and for flying from Europe to do them; and to Caroline Velik for her beautiful styling (especially for putting a brick in a photo); and, of course, thank you to all the Murdoch Books team—you rock.

I'm so grateful, so many, many thanks.

MATT
xx

287

NOTES

NOTES

ISBN: 978-1-57912-934-7

Library of Congress Cataloging-in-Publication Data on file at the offices
of Black Dog & Leventhal Publishers, Inc.

Manufactured in China

Published by Black Dog & Leventhal Publishers, Inc.
151 West 19th Street
New York, New York 10011

Distributed by Workman Publishing Company
225 Varick Street
New York, New York 10014

h g f e d c b a